SIMPLY QUIT DRINKING

AN INSPIRATIONAL JOURNEY
FROM NEAR DEATH

Words of Praise

"Karen, I had fond memories about you. You were always very helpful, caring and warm. I do recall memories that you were a little off; I didn't know that was due to alcoholism. You must have hidden it so well from me. I admire your courage in writing a book about this, and I am happy that you have started a great life."

Susan Zhou
Reston, VA
Friend and former roommate

"Karen, I am so super proud of you for writing this book, for you and for others who may be struggling. I know it has to be a little uncomfortable stepping out like this -- but you did!"

Connie Mayes
Richmond, VA
Friend and former coworker

SIMPLY QUIT DRINKING

AN INSPIRATIONAL JOURNEY
FROM NEAR DEATH

BY

KAREN GREGG PRICE
AND
JOSEPH F. PRICE

Reaching Peak LLC
www.ReachingPeak.com
Contact@ReachingPeak.com

Published by:
Reaching Peak LLC
Apollo Beach, FL

The authors of this book do not dispense medical advice or prescribe the use of any technique as a form of treatment for physical or medical problems without the advice of a physician, either directly or indirectly. The intent of the authors is only to offer information of a general nature to help you. In the event you use any of the information in this book for yourself, the authors and the publisher assume no responsibility for your actions.

Audio Book Available at **www.ReachingPeak. com** and **www.SimplyQuitDrinking.com.** Invite others to take the Quit Drinking Challenge at **www.SimpleChallenge.com.**

Tune in to **ReachingPeakShow.com** for inspirational talk radio. Invite us to speak at your event by visiting ReachingSpeakers.com.

ISBN 978-0-9816134-0-6

Printed in the United States of America

DEDICATIONS

This book is dedicated with love to my daughter, Savanna, for being my blessing; to my husband, Joseph, for not giving up; and to my family, Stephanie, Kevin, Jon, Mom and Dad, for loving me enough.

ACKNOWLEDGEMENTS

Thank you, God, for keeping me alive to be here today.

Thank you to my husband, Joseph F. Price, for agreeing to this book, and enduring the pain of rehashing this emotional ordeal, in for others to experience and learn from.

Thank you to my big sister, Stephanie Kuhns, for loving me enough that you took me on as an additional burden when you really couldn't. You listened to my cry for help.

Thank you to my brothers, Kevin Kish and Jon Kish, for loving me enough that you also came to my rescue, even though it disrupted your own lives.

Thank you to my parents, Thomas and Charlotte Gregg, for all your help and support after I became sober.

Thanks to the entire family, friends, and community for all your help with the arrival and first year of baby Savanna.

Thank you to my best friends from middle school, Lana Chiariello and Jenny (Lambert) Courchene, who I first told about my problematic years, planting the seed for this book.

Thank you to all the hospital doctors, nurses, and health-care workers, Baylife and A.C.T.S, and lawmakers.

Thank you to Dr. David Sheehan, for studying Anxiety disorders in an effort to continue to improve peoples' lives.

Most of all, thank you to my daughter, Savanna, the most beautiful love I've ever known. I'm so very delighted that you are here. I love you.

Table of Contents

Part 1 - My Story

I Nearly Died   5
My Drinking Problem   7
Becoming Physically Dependant on the Drug Alcohol   13
The Embarrassment at Work   21
Big Trouble in Sweet Virginia   27
Hospitalizations for Alcohol Poisoning   31
The Beginning of My Long, Relapsing Recovery   35
Mental Health Laws   41
My Spiritual Awakening   45
The Longest Functional   49
Blackout   49

Part 2 - Recovery

A Major Turning Point   53
Staying In When the Going Got Tough   57
My Big Reason to Quit   61

Part 3 - How I Quit Drinking

I Simply Quit Drinking   67
Alcoholics Anonymous:
A Spiritual Foundation for Recovery –Twelve Steps   71
My Trademark Technique – Mindset Reversion   75
The Drug Alcohol – Not the Best Medicine for Anxiety   79
Personal Development   81
How Joseph Learned to Help   85

Part 4- Loving an Alcoholic - by Joseph Price

Loving an Alcoholic   89
How I Helped My Wife Simply Quit Drinking   99
Epilogue   101
References

FOREWORD

By Stephanie Kuhns, sister

Never during your alcoholism did I ever take it serious enough. I'd like to pass on to anyone reading your book... that just because you still love an alcoholic, and just because you still enjoy talking to your alcoholic even when they are drunk (and you end up hanging up on them because they won't remember anyway), does not mean that that individual isn't near death! Our brother, Kevin, knew from the very beginning that you were going to die if you did't stop drinking to excess. He also knew that any drinking would always lead to excessive drinking. That you cannot have just a bit, just tonight, ever. Someone else's story touched Kevin to the point that he pushed me into getting involved with you.

I realized you were near death when you flew into Tampa, and I picked you up at curbside, with my kids in the back seat. I took one look at you walking up to the car and realized that you looked exactly like our father, on his deathbed, in the hospital who had died ten years prior from alcoholism. If you recall, we went to see him in Cleveland, and went back to Grandpa's house We went home to Indiana, and Dad died within a week of multiple organ failure. I could also see that you were so severely depressed, yet physically couldn't break free from the chemical dependency, despite your true intentions and desires to do so.

You came home to see me, so I could see what was going on. You didn't necessarily do it intentionally, but you knew somewhere inside of you that you had to do it. You knew I would care and help.

The worst part of it all was that even though I didn't want to see this day to day destruction of your life. I also didn't want you close enough to have to care. I wanted to care, but with two small children, I didn't have the luxury of being able to care.

I do thank God that He put Joseph into our lives. If not for Joseph working with Kevin and I, you would have never started your road to recovery. I truly believe that with no one near you to care, you would have sunk even lower. You would have made it home eventually, but would there have been time to save you?

After your visit, I called Kevin and Jon within a few weeks (you got arrested again). That was pivotal. Had you not come home, and I hadn't seen your physical status, I would have never called our brothers. I don't know why or when, but sometime during the few weeks after your trip here, I called you and you gave the phone to Joseph. That was pivotal as well. Had he not talked to me then, I don't know where we would be today. I went out on a limb to ask for his help, not knowing him, and he accepted against his better judgment. He knew you would not give in easily, and you'd perceive that working with your family was in essence going behind your back. Yet, Joseph had the courage to do it anyway. He saw in you what we all knew was there, but it must have been next to impossible to for him to really believe you had it in you, considering the way you were living.

I love you, Karen. Give yourself credit for what you did. You are an enormously strong individual. You have always been driven and successful.

The truth is hard to tell and even harder to see in person as I did. I watched you torment yourself for at least 2-3 years. I think the real story of Karen will make anyone who knows you cry to know what you went through. I know there is a really moving story in these pages. I am just afraid to read it.

Love, Steph

INTRODUCTION

The worst advice I've ever gotten, without a doubt, was to cure a hangover with alcohol. The saying was presented to me innocently enough. They said the cure to a hangover is to get a hair off the tail of the dog that bit you.

That saying can directly be translated into, if drinking hurts, drink some more to feel better. If I had only suffered through every hangover in the morning, and kept my "no drinking before noon" rule, maybe I would have been safe. As a young person, please never follow that advice. My body hurt for a reason. Take the hangover pain as a signal. It's better to learn to quit drinking and have a better tomorrow. Better yet, don't start drinking alcohol. I will share the path it led to for me, and hopefully my story is reason enough not to cross the line.

My life began as promising and rewarding, then led to sickness and wasted years. Only by the grace of God, am I alive and free again. I learned no matter how smart, good-looking, nice, and hard-working a person is, that doesn't preclude alcohol from destroying their life. I went to the deep trenches of alcoholism, beat the odds, and made it out. Luckily, I am much better off having been through the misery and distress. Those difficult years were the greatest problem I have ever faced. The years after were the greatest challenge, and also the most precious. I probably should be dead, except that there must be a reason I've been spared, perhaps for this book to help others. I am more humble and grateful, have a new found love of life, and *each and every day I'm winning*.

2

Part 1

My Story

Chapter 1

I Nearly Died

Finally, after years of uncontrolled drinking, I became serious about quitting drinking alcohol. It was ruining my life. I looked sickly at a moderatly young age of only 35. Alcohol ruled my life, and I was deeply tired of it. I never knew, though, that when a person is totally physically dependant on alcohol, they can't just stop cold turkey. It can kill them.

I hadn't had a drink in days, and I went to a family gathering with my boyfriend at the time. Socializing, I was standing up normal one moment, and the next moment I was down on the floor. Here's what I remember. Out of no where, my head snapped and jerked all the way left as if some voodoo doll somewhere was conducting my motions. Still very conscious of my surroundings, I was utterly shocked and scared that my body was acting on its own. It wasn't my thoughts or brain controlling my movement anymore. Both my arms started shaking and flapping uncontrollably. My arms were waiving up and down like I was pretending to be a chicken. I was petrified; and I couldn't stop what was happening to me. Then I was down for the count, and the world went black. Then, I didn't feel or think anything. Like the flick of a switch, I was turned off. All the while I was unconscious, not breathing, and seconds turned into more than a minute, as I started dying.

Later I would find out, after my trip to the hospital, that I went unconscious, stopped breathing, turned blue, and my jaw had locked shut so I could not breathe. To my blessing, my boyfriend at the time was an Army-trained nurse. First, he used his hands to try to open my mouth so I could breathe. My teeth clamped down on his fingers, slicing open his skin. Retreating, he shouted for a spoon to the room of onlookers. Once in hand, he shoved the metal spoon into my mouth, scratching and chipping a tooth, to pry my jaws open, force my tongue out of the way, and allow me to breathe. They told me I didn't breathe for quite a long time. I awoke for only a short period of time bumping along in the ambulance with its bright lights and siren carrying me away. I had no idea what had happened. He saved my life. Thank you and may God bless you C.L.

After that I was always afraid I would have an alcohol withdrawal seizure, so I would drink enough everyday to make sure I didn't. I also kept a popsicle stick next to my bed. When I met Joseph, my future husband, a few months later, in July 2005, I would explain to him that the popsicle stick was there so that if I ever had another alcohol withdrawal seizure, he would need to pry my mouth open for me to breathe, and then call 911.

Chapter 2

My Drinking Problem

If a person never starts drinking, they won't drink, and they'll have absolutely no chance of being an alcoholic. It's very simple. However, most Americans have tried their first drink of alcohol by age 16.

My family wasn't the beginning of my drinking. I rarely recall my parents ever drinking. From here on out that means my birth mother and my step-father that adopted me. He is the only father I've known, and he has been my father since I was seven years old. We did not attend church, and when I was growing up I don't think I ever saw a copy of the Bible in the house. I was spiritually ignorant in every way. When I was a younger child though, when we lived with Grandma and Grandpa, and when we did go to church, I was baptized in the Lutheran church at the young age of six years old. I don't remember much about back then, but I have photographs of my brothers and my sister and I all dressed up to go to Sunday school. We lived with my grandparents and Mom, since our natural father had left us.

I had a very healthy living environment that didn't include copious amounts of drinking. Not until I was a teenager, did I want to find out what drinking was like. I really only did it because in just playing around, my sister and I had snuck aboard a boat and taken a large bottle of Canadian Whiskey. Drinking was supposed to be fun. The first time I drank alcohol, I drank a Big Gulp™ cup full of straight Whiskey in one evening. A bunch of kids from high school got together and drove sneaking into the back of the drive in movie theatre in St. Petersburg, Florida, where we lived. I got terribly sick and recall throwing up with my head hanging out the window of the car at about 45 mph.

I recall my parents being out of town for once. Since we lived on a sailboat, rather than waking up the next morning on a front lawn, I awoke on the dock of the St. Petersburg Marina with people walking by and over me. Thinking back, I wonder why they didn't ask me if I was okay. Later in life these kinds of things would involve an ambulance, and likely the police, at my door or yard.

My sister, Stephanie, and I had stashed the bottle of whiskey under my bed. One of my older adult brothers found out and told Mom and Dad. The bottle was confiscated, and we were put on restriction. I must say that restriction wasn't much different from every other day. I had a disciplined upbringing. I didn't use the phone to call friends, and I didn't hang out with friends. We were kept busy with school, housework, and other work projects.

After that, I didn't do much more drinking in high school except for cutting class a few times to go to party with other kids who somehow had access to alcohol and a home to go to party in. That was most likely possible due to an irresponsible parent or adult. In my senior year I got into a little trouble for missing every Friday for several weeks and forging my own notes that were obviously not well written. I graduated in 1988, and spent the next six weeks of the summer bicycle racing in Europe. When I returned, I went just across Tampa Bay to college at the University of South Florida. I was a complete amateur at dating, since I had not dated in high school at all. I met a

8

very handsome guy, who I dated for four years. He didn't drink. That was a blessing!

Around that time my biological father died. Our family got a call that Dad was in the hospital, dying from alcoholism. I recall going to Ohio and seeing him in a hospital bed. His color was awful and it looked painful and difficult for him to even move. I was afraid to get close to him. I don't remember, but I don't think I went to his bedside. I just looked at everyone else from across the room. My brothers and sister were by his side as he lay there looking very ill and trying to talk. It's clear to me that I blocked out a lot of memory around that hospital visit, and I don't even know exactly what day he passed away. I'm told it was about a week later. I wasn't sure what to think of it all.

The really weird thing is that I've said more than a handful of times in the past that "I've never had someone close to me die." Only now that I'm writing this, I realize I have. I've just blocked out most of the pain and memory. I've never thought about it much. I will say this though, as I wrote this down, I cried and stopped writing for a moment.

If I could tell my dead father anything, it would be this. I forgive you for leaving us kids and Mom. I know you probably regret that. I am not surprised that someone can drink themselves to death. If I didn't have something to care about that mattered enough now, I might still be a depressed and selfish alcoholic on my way to dying. I wish I could have helped you.

Now that I've wiped my tears away, let me go on and tell how I got through my first couple years after my natural father's death. I did keep a few house rules when I was about eighteen to twenty years old. The rules were to not keep alcohol in the house, not drink before noon, and only drink when I was happy and celebrating. I'm sure I read somewhere that the opposite would indicate problem drinking, so I kept away from breaking those rules. I didn't know at the time that those few little rules kept me from going into very dangerous territory.

I managed to get a fake ID with someone's help when I was twenty. I hit the night club scene full on. One night, at the entrance to a hip Tampa bar, I got questioned as they tried to figure out if that ID was really mine. They asked me what my birth sign was. I hadn't studied up, and I got caught by the police officer at the door. I giggled, not knowing how serious it was. He could have sent me to jail that night. The nice officer didn't do that, but he sent me home and kept the fake ID. That was one of the best things that happened to me with regard to drinking. I couldn't purchase alcohol or go to dance clubs for the next few months until I turned twenty-one, so I stayed home and studied my college books.

I had always been athletic, in non-team sports like running. When I got back from bicycle racing in Europe, I was entirely sick of it and traded in my bike at a pawn shop. I picked up a pair of jogging shoes, and I ran for fitness every day. At that time, running was just something I did to stay in shape, of course it made me feel good too.

I held a job, most of the time being a bank teller or receptionist. I was fairly happy, but not very social. I didn't like to go do anything because I didn't have any friends, and I really didn't know how to find friends. Growing up, my sister made many friends, so I just tagged along with her entourage. It was very hard for me to socialize even though I would always hear that I'm such a very nice, likeable person.

I started drinking again as soon as I was legally allowed. The only people I knew were people I met when I was out drinking. The people I called "friends" were not people I went to the mall with or studied with, they were people who I'd see at the night clubs any night of the week that I was out drinking. By the way, this is a strong indica-

10

tor that a person's life is not balanced or healthy if all your friends are drinking most of the time. I was using alcohol as a prescription drug for me to be able to socialize and overcome anxiety. I didn't know at the time that I was using alcohol as a non-prescription drug for me to self-medicate, so that I would be able to socialize and overcome anxiety.

Being an intelligent person and a "low price" shopper at the time, I discovered ways to get "more bang for my buck" when it came to alcohol. The alcohol content of a beverage is measured by the percentage of alcohol by volume of liquid. That means, if a person buys wine, they get more alcohol than if they buy beer. I can recite the alcohol content of almost any beer, wine, or liquor. I shopped for groceries at a store that shows the price per ounce on the shelf for every product, and I still shop at the same place, now 37 years old. When the "ice" beer brands came out, I was in heaven. I bought the beer with the most alcohol per volume in it. That was smart shopping to me.

When I was drinking, I was a bunch of fun. My party friends will say that I was fun to watch and usually just a tad out of control. I never kept it at a simple few drinks and just having some nice conversation about whatever people talk about at parties. I don't know what people talk about at parties, and every time I get invited to one, I start to worry days ahead about what I will say or talk about. The anxiety builds to the point that I really wouldn't even want to go, because I felt I would have nothing to say, or what I would say will be way different from everyone else.

I had found what I thought to be a best friend, but what my husband calls a "friendly enemy," when I started drinking and clubbing. We were so called "friends" for a long time, like 15 years I'd guess. The only thing we ever did was party. Having already graduated from college, she was earning a lot of money. For years she would pick up the tab, and even pay for my plane tickets to go just about

11

anywhere with her because I was so much fun when I was drinking. Imagine that, being an entertaining drinker could really get me places!

I thought that as long as I kept my rules, and I was just a night partier, I was okay. However, I came up with problem drinking ways during this time period that didn't break my small rule set. I took an alcohol "self test" and decided I wasn't an alcoholic and that I didn't have a problem with alcohol.

Chapter 3

Becoming Physically Dependant on the Drug Alcohol

There is obviously a gap in self tests. My life confirms that, and I'll be the first one to say that the self test missed helping me.

There are all kinds of self tests for identifying a problem drinker. Just search the Internet for words like "alcoholic self test." I'm sure I took a similar self test at one point in college. At the time, I positively answered many of the questions that pointed toward the potential to have a problem with alcohol. For example, I recall that I confirmed that I would have a drink at home before going to a party to ease my nerves. I also confirmed that I would usually have more than a couple drinks in one evening. However, I thought I was safe because there were plenty of questions that I answered "no" to like that I didn't drink at home alone or to cure a low mood swing feeling. I really thought or convinced myself that I was safe. I had no idea where I was headed later in life.

There are several widely recognized alcohol abuse self-tests such as AUDIT, the Alcohol Use Disorders Identication Test, the Michigan Alcoholism Screening Test

(MAST), and the CAGE test. MAST can identify 98% of "alcoholics," defined as patients who are physically harmed or dependant – "but less than half of those with alcohol problems of a lesser degree"[1].The CAGE test is similarly targeted at dependent users. The problem with these tests is that those whom could benefit the most with counseling are not found or counseled. Like me, many slip past until the time comes in their life that triggers the heavy drinking, and we quickly slip into physical dependence.

Here is the CAGE test:
1. Have you ever felt you should Cut down on your drinking?
2. Have people Annoyed you by criticizing your drinking?
3. Have you ever felt bad or Guilty about your drinking?
4. Have you ever had a drink first thing in the morning to steady nerves or get rid of a hangover?

Two or three affirmative answers are highly suspicious and would indicate that a person is poised to have a drinking problem if they don't already. If a person answers "yes" to any of these, and they don't think they have a problem with drinking, then I think they are in denial or unaware of how close they've come to having a life-altering problem. If a person gives a "yes" to all four questions, they are pinpointed as an alcoholic.

By the way, the acronym CAGE comes from four words within the questions in this order: "Cut down," "Annoyed," "Guilty," and "Eye Opener," "Eye opener" isn't actually in the words of number four, but I think that it is the biggest indicator of problem drinking and alcoholism. For most of my life, I could answer "no" to three of these questions. Only the first one, did I answer "yes" to, which is that it had crossed my mind a few times to cut down on drinking.

I was able to finish college twice. I completed my

14

Bachelor of Arts degree in mass communications, public relations, with a minor in sociology, when I was twenty-five (1995). Then I completed my Master of Business Administration degree when I was twenty-eight. I landed a pretty good job at a software company doing marketing. I was a great worker and I enjoyed working. I met my first husband-to-be, and moved across the state of Florida. I landed an even better job as a Product Manager in a "dot-com" company.

Sometimes I felt I should cut down a little on my drinking. Mostly I meant that on an evening of going out partying with my husband at the time, and his friends, that I'd always get a little more drunk than was good for me. It definitely included a hangover, but nothing I couldn't suffer through the next day. Usually that was a weekend day anyway. Please note that I said we partied with "his friends." I'm still working on getting myself to go do things with friends that don't include a drink. As it turns out, I have just a touch of Generalized Anxiety Disorder. Many people who suffer from anxiety disorders drink, and can become alcoholics. Alcohol is a legal drug that eases the symptoms of anxiety.

There is a point at which a problem drinker becomes physically dependent on alcohol in order to function. It's a silent transition. "You've got alcoholism" doesn't show up in someone's inbox nor does a certified letter arrive stating the line has been crossed to becoming officially an alcoholic. Since I just wrote about tests, I'll continue by letting on that blood tests are quite accurate at showing problem drinking or worse. A blood test can show a person who has a physical dependency on alcohol, or liver or other organ and physiological damage. Later in life, the results of a blood test, clearly put to me by a stern nurse would scare me enough to really think about what I was doing to my body.

I'm sure the slow progression to physical dependence happens in different ways for problem drinkers. For me, I can trace it to three important events.

Even though I partied a little harder than most on the weekend, and I was usually the last one to stop drinking in a late evening. I had a single coworker of mine who often invited me to go out dancing during the week, including some heavy drinking. While that was okay for her, it wasn't okay for me. Actually, it turns out she had just as bad a problem as I did.

It just so happens that I was at my peak of physical fitness at that point in my life. I just finished months of training, and I ran my first and only marathon – the Disney Marathon in 2002. At thirty-two years old, I was "healthy as a horse" as they say. I ran the twenty-six point two miles in four hours and twenty-three minutes. I felt great, and I was physically and mentally at my peak. Note that I don't mention being spiritually peaked. I now know that I was spiritually bankrupt.

As I said, I can pinpoint the events that influenced me in crossing the alcoholic line. Along with my heredity and socialization, there were three events that changed me forever. The first major event was that I was laid off during the dot com bubble burst January 1, 2002. It was devastating to me. I tried for a long time to find work. I resorted to looking for any kind of job. I couldn't seem to find another decent job in software product management in that area of Florida, and my husband at the time wanted me to take a job doing anything. I knew I wouldn't be satisfied doing just anything. While I was job searching, I was told to take the "MBA" off my resume and I'd have a better shot.

My ever increasing boredom lead to depression, and I started drinking during the day at home while I blazed the Internet seeking employment and applying to countless jobs. I carefully hid the cheap Mad Dog 20/20 in a cardboard box in my office at home. After 10 months of searching, I landed another software product manager

16

position and we moved to the beautiful state of Virginia. No more hidden daytime drinking. I was back at work and enjoying life, and I was back to running daily again.

Moving to another state can be very difficult on a marriage, let alone a single person. Let me be blunt, it was hard for me to make friends unless I drank. I was always getting invited through coworkers to go out and socialize. I went out occasionally with people after work, but my husband didn't. I have to admit the 'crew' from work was not typical. In fact, they were quite wild, more so than the people I had been around in Florida. Couple-sharing and married people making indiscretions that I would have never thought they were capable of doing were the norm. No wonder my husband at the time didn't want to go out with them. To me they were interesting and fun. Eventually, we went down the path to divorce at my request. I was a different person, and going out drinking allowed me to be away from my husband far too much. It was a hasty decision to get divorced, and my life began spiraling downward starting with depression. I didn't like being single again actually.

The second major influencing event happened when I found myself to be a newly single person. I did what most newly single women do, and I focused on losing a little weight and making myself look better. I started the Atkins diet. What part did the Atkins diet have to do with stimulating a problem drinker to go places she'd never gone with her drinking before? The diet introduced me to "low-carbohydrate" drinking.

I was working hard, in fact it was the most stressful job I've ever had. I was running daily, and started eating protein and fat only as the diet prescribes. I kept my carbohydrates low. The diet says to keep carbohydrates intake down to 20 grams per day. While starting the diet it says strictly not to drink. Right up front the diet says that the person must make a lifetime commitment to it. I was willing to do that to keep in a size 4. The funny thing is that I thought the drinking part was not allowed at all. Four weeks into the diet, wearing a size 2 and weighing 109 pounds (4'11"), I was getting a lot of male attention.

The crux of the second important event was that I found out from a coworker that I was allowed to drink after the "induction period" of the Atkins diet, and specifically I could drink vodka and gin. I had never been a person to drink liquor, mostly wine and beer. However, those two liquors are the alcohol beverages lowest in carbohydrates. I further went on to read that I could have gin and tonic, preferably diet tonic. The sum of carbohydrates in a gin and tonic drink is very low. So, once past the induction period, and the diet allows an increase carbohydrate intake a bit, a gin and tonic drink fits right in. In my mind that meant I could stay thin and still have fun drinking and socializing.

Gin and tonic drinking led to drinking other liquors. I had grown to really enjoy "Appletinis," which is an apple-flavored martini. There was a bar in Leesburg that had an entire menu of martinis. That's where I had my first martini ever, with my boss and coworkers. Imagine that; up until I was 33 years old, I'd never had a martini. That became my favorite and propelled me to yet another level upwards to becoming an alcoholic. Needless to say, I kept that under control as I always had and did a good job not letting drinking interfere with my high paying stress-filled job. Then I quit my job. Now I was all alone and had no job.

Now living alone, I had an unsatisfying long distance relationship, and the stress at work had been crazy. I had enough money to quit and do nothing. In my mind I was going to travel, and then go back to work after a few months. In the back of my mind I knew I would probably move back to my home city, Tampa, Florida, and be closer to my family. For the next 8 months, I did do a lot of traveling. I immediately went on a cruise to Nova Scotia.

Regardless of what amount of money I had in the bank, I was always "cheap." It was how I grew up, and it had a lot to do with how I kept and saved money. So, to keep up my regular diet, I brought along drinking water bottles filled with gin, and I didn't bring any tonic. That would have been too much to bring in my suitcases and get it aboard without problems. I learned to just drink gin straight, the lime-flavored products helped. Aboard the ship it was party time just about 24 hours a day if desired. I was like a kid going off to college. There was no reason not to just drink all the time. There was no one to stop me either. I was alone and having a great time. A week later when I got off the ship, I kept up the drinking.

I wasn't really looking for a job too hard, and I had nothing but time and money. I traveled to many cities in the U.S. I had continued my little trick of bringing gin or vodka in drinking water bottles. I had many nights I don't remember. Deep down I was depressed as a single person. The dating wasn't going well. Now that I look back, dating probably would have gone a lot better without drinking. I know now that my drinking was slightly over the top, and the guys I dated were probably turned off by that. Intelligent, cute and shapely, I had a lot going for me.

On a skiing trip with my sister's family at Breckenridge, I got drunk and planted myself on the lobby couch at the resort. The police were called because no one could wake me up. When I came to, they questioned me, and thankfully I was able to answer who I was and who I was staying with. My brother-in-law got a wake up call, and he was summoned to come claim me. He was quite disturbed with my behavior, especially since they had a small child at that time, and I was an adult acting like an embarrassing fool.

Just a few days later, the last day of the week-long ski trip, I went snowboarding by myself. On my last run down the mountain, at the very bottom, I was coming up behind a father and his two little children. I slowed to not hit them and fell. I put my arms down to catch myself, landing on a hard block of ice. All I felt was a snap.

I'd never broken a bone before. Generally, I pass out when I even just see a needle. I didn't feel any pain at all. Not because of any alcohol, but because I immediately went into shock. I looked down, and holding my mitten covered arm out, I could see a strange shape that didn't look like my normal arm. It looked like I had quite a big bend near my wrist. When I finally did get help 15 minutes later, I insisted that they not remove the mitten. I was afraid to see what was underneath. I still find it very interesting that I didn't feel any pain whatsoever.

The important point of breaking my arm is that it kept me from my running routine for the next couple months. Running was always my most effective outlet for stress, and it allowed me to calm my nerves and do a lot of meditative thinking. It may have been one of the biggest parts of my life that kept me from going over the edge. However, I never picked up daily running again. Still single, I landed myself into a couple bad relationships, usually still involving dating with drinking. I felt that nothing could make me happy, and I found that drinking would allow me to not mind. For the first time in my life, I was drinking morning, noon, and night. Nobody stopped me. I wasn't sober long enough to realize how bad off I was. Not having friends too close to me helped, because there really wasn't anybody who cared too much. I was living off of my 401k after saving diligently for years.

I sold my home from the marriage and moved. I rented the bottom floor of a big townhouse in Reston, Virginia, so I basically had my own apartment. I kept a large bottle of apple-flavored vodka next to the side of the couch. I didn't bother with mixing anything. I drank straight from the liter.

Chapter 4

The Embarrassment at Work

Realizing my savings wouldn't last forever, and getting a little nervous about taking care of myself, I tried to work. I would land a job, and try to stop drinking, but my body would fight me, trembling so that I couldn't even write. I felt sick all the time when I couldn't drink. I threw up going home from an interview. At one interview the guy said something to me about a "funny smell" in the room. Looking back, of course now I know what he meant —I reeked of alcohol. I was oblivious to the smell of alcohol on my breath and my body all the time.

I remember I landed a job in Washington, D.C., and on my first day of work I had to go home sick. I threw up in the bathroom after excusing myself from a conversation with my new manager. Then I asked to leave, complaining of a bad stomach ache or something. They told me not to come back at all.

I guess on paper I still looked like a great candidate who simply said she'd been traveling a lot (true), but that couldn't explain the increasingly long period of time out of work. I also couldn't explain how many jobs I lost and couldn't tell anyone about it. I couldn't explain why my references were from so long ago. I didn't want to ask my old references anymore anyway, and I had no way to know if they were really tired of vouching for me. I couldn't keep track of who I put down as a reference so many times.

My body was completely dependant on alcohol. I tried to quit drinking on my own, and during those tough days my whole body would shake and sweat through the night. My muscles would cramp up from a lack of nutrients. My head hurt. I felt like my worst hangover times ten or twenty. I'd also compare it to a very bad flu. The muscle cramping really hurt, and it continuously woke me throughout the night.

I often think back and I remember all the people around me who I thought didn't know how much I drank. Only now do I know the signals that were there. As the alcoholic, I couldn't realize how ill I had become, because it became normal. Drinking becomes a daily activity, like eating or brushing teeth, or not brushing in the case of some alcoholics. It is ingrained into the day as if it were nothing too abnormal. It becomes more of an unconscious decision, like taking a vitamin.

If just one friend would have told me straight to my face that I clearly had a problem, and how ridiculous it had become, that probably would have helped. I realize now that a former co-worker of mine tried to tell me. It was the closest thing I ever heard from anyone to telling me I had a problem. She said, "We're here for you. We all care about you."

At the time, I had no idea what she was talking about. Now that I'm sober, I will remember her forever for getting the closest to telling me to get help, with the exception of my family and the day I went to rehab. I hope if she reads this book, it fills her soul with joy to know that she took a very risky step to try to connect with me. She tried to help me, rather than right me off and make fun of me. Thank you, L.C.

Yes, some of my coworkers thought it was funny. At work we had instant messaging and I'm sure now that it was full of poking fun about my problem. One time, in a celebration meeting where we were having cake at the office, someone asked loudly from across the room of 25 others what was in my water bottle I was drinking. At that time in particular it was just flavored water. However, the comment stuck with me forever. It was embarrassing defending myself in a room full of people. What was the worst part was that he didn't come to me, one on one, and try saying something like this: "We should talk. I've noticed you might be having some trouble, do you have a minute?" He made a jab at me across a room full of people. What was the purpose of his comment? I'm a nice person, and I certainly didn't respond to him with "why are you so fat?" I simply defended my water bottle and myself and acted like it wasn't a big deal.

If I were that person, what would I have accomplished by making that insinuation in front of so many people? It was an outright statement that could only deliver pain and embarrassment. If I were one of the other people in the room, how would I have felt? Would I have felt sorry for me? Would I have thought his comment was funny? Would I have felt embarrassed and try to cover up the dead air by saying something positive?

There are things that can be done in a situation like that to help. I know, if I were someone else in the room that day, I would have given him an evil look, and then with a big smile said, "Let's eat some cake, isn't it good." Later, I'd go talk to that person as if I knew nothing and just try to get close enough to eventually gain their trust, hoping sometime they would tell me about it.

What really surprises me is the big gaping hole where the company I worked for didn't help. I was an employee of a company that had seven buildings on a huge campus. I had health coverage. Not one person suggested I see a human resources person. No manager set up a meeting for me with human resources. No one did a thing. They

23

wrote me off and waited to get rid of me, I guess. I was struggling with my addiction, but rather than get me help, they just continued to give me my paycheck. Eight weeks at my rate of pay could have paid for a 30-day rehab. How did so many people turn their heads away, laugh, and do nothing is the question I continually ask myself.

Money was not an issue at that time. I was able to buy a little condo in Herndon, and I still had some savings. If that company could afford to pay me so much per week to provide some of my worst work, why couldn't they come to terms with me? Why didn't they address the problem and give me a chance to go get help. I also wonder to this day why the company didn't allow me to return to my job if I came back guaranteed 'clean and sober'.

Under the pressure of the increasingly difficult-to-hide heavy drinking, I crumbled. I hopped a plain on a Wednesday night and flew to Tampa to be near my family. Not thinking clearly, I was having a peak of anxiety and still very much under the influence of alcohol. I sent an email to my boss saying that I needed a couple days off. I stayed at my brother's house. What was interesting is that before he picked me up, he and his wife made an effort and removed almost every bottle of liquor from the house. I found one beer in the fridge one night and drank it. They didn't know that not letting me drink could have caused a withdrawal seizure. I didn't know that at the time either. I made it through several days. My brother tried to talk to me. I had finally checked my messages on my phone. Apparently my boss said that I had "abandoned my job" and left without notice. My brother encouraged me on Monday morning to call each person, and try to talk about keeping my job. I talked to my manager, his manager, a Vice President, and a human resources representative. My manager and human resources had the final say, and they decided to terminate me for abandoning my job.

I went back to Virginia anyway later in the day

Monday. I was depressed and lonely. My career was going down the drain, and so was my body... I threw up all the time. I drank all the time. In fact, I couldn't eat anymore. I couldn't bear swallowing food. I just couldn't get a morsel down my throat, so I sustained myself on soup, juice, and alcohol.

Surprisingly, as much as I loved the Internet, I never looked up "alcoholism," "rehabilitation," "alcoholics anonymous" or any words like that. I just figured no one cared, so I wouldn't care either. I had no real responsibilities to anyone except myself. I didn't have a care in the world when I drank. I didn't mind if I died. I even asked God to let me go away from this planet. What I didn't realize was that after losing my job, everything would get much worse. The repercussions were huge. I was really hurting my family. My "friends" were scared for me. I was allowing myself to start to die.

I lived a risky life in that I was always under the influence of alcohol. I would black out often. The problem is that I don't remember a lot of things. This is the scariest story I'll ever tell about being blacked out. I vaguely remember having been blacked out, then coming to find a man in the passenger seat of my car and I was driving. I remember thinking he had a gun, and that I was not sure how he got in my car or where I was driving. I faded in and out of consciousness. At one moment I realized I was in a house. Scared beyond words, I extreme flight mode, I found myself quickly scanning the room for an exit door and my keys. He was slender and about 5' 8." I reached upward with my curled fist, sticking it up into this man's jaw and neck. I said to him, "Do you want to die today?" Then, releasing him, in a flash I ran across the room, grabbed my keys, and jetted out the door. I don't remember anything else, not getting home, or the next day, not anything.

I've been told since then what else had occurred. Once outside, I called the police. The police should have arrested me for driving under the influence, but I wasn't in my car. The very kind Montgomery County police were concerned about my being a victim of an assault. Instead of arresting me, and considering the circumstances I had described to them, the police called Joseph, and he came to pick me up.

Thinking very lowly of myself, I made my life so that I was not responsible for anyone or anything on the planet. I had no children, no pets, and no close friends. That way, I was insuring myself a life that would enable drinking as much and as often as I wanted without any repercussions. To me, at the time, I didn't really think. I just drank.

Chapter 5

Big Trouble in Sweet Virginia

In some states, one can get arrested for an old law on the books called "public drunkenness." In Virginia, if someone is arrested for public drunkenness, on the citation and invitation to court it says it's for "public swearing or intoxication." That's right, "public swearing" is included.

During my two years of living in Virginia, I was arrested twice for "public swearing and intoxication." Let that be a lesson to you. I got out of it on one occasion because I was taking Klonopin, a prescription drug, and nowhere on the pharmacy print out of information did it say not to drink. I just brought that paper into court, and that was forgiven. In Virginia, the police can arrest a person for simply swearing.

The law 18.2-388 says "profane swearing and intoxication in public; penalty: transportation of public inebriates to detoxification center." If a person curses or swears or is intoxicated in public, an officer can arrest them and transport them to a detoxification center. It's a Class 4 misdemeanor with two fines, one in cash, and one in embarrassment!

There has been a lot of press in Virginia about the

"profane swearing and intoxication in public" law and how it is enforced. The police have waited outside a bar for people to come out and arrest them on the spot. Where I live, Fairfax County, the police even go into the bar to arrest. A bar in Virginia is considered a public place.

As I left a bar in Reston Town Center, I got arrested and carried off to jail. I was pissed off and also scared, but I was still drunk. I also have a great sense of humor. When I was arrested, the officer hadn't put my handcuffs on very tight. Then, while I was riding along in the back of the police car, I realized I could squeeze my hands out of the cuffs! Well, rather than just take the cuffs off and try to make a run for it when the time was right, I found that the time would not ever be right. It was a really stupid plan anyway, and as far as I knew the police are not allowed to shoot someone in the back while running away unarmed. They'd have to catch me. Regardless, that plan would fail because when I got taken to the station, the police pulled the cruiser into a large garage and closed the garage exit door before I got invited out of the back seat of the car.

Seeing this coming, I decided to just have a little fun. I removed one hand from one cuff, but I made it look like my cuffs were still secure. When I was let out of the back of the cruiser, I threw my hands up into the air, wiggled and shook, and made a silly shrill "lad-da-bla-bla-bla" noise ending with a hard laugh. Flailing my arms was probably not too smart. To a trained officer, that was behavior that could have looked like I pulled something out of my pocket and was waving it, or to say the least, that I was out of control and a danger. The next thing I know, there were about six or more officers dashing through a door coming into the garage! It was just little me waiving my arms around and having some fun, since I was going to jail anyway. Needless to say, that got quite a few officers upset that evening.

I was really afraid they were going to put me in that

28

general population cell like seen on TV. I was afraid I'd be in the big cell where I might get beat up or harassed to say the least, or maybe some big woman would want me! I remember it took about four officers to get my mug shot. One officer had put on latex gloves and held my jaw so that my face would point at the camera. Lucky for me, I was such a handful that they gave me my own "suite," also known as a cell, with my own toilet and my own bed. "Thank you, Lord," I panted, still short of breathe from all the excitement and wrestling around for the mug shot. I'm sure when the alcohol wore off and I was in a room with 20 other women I'd probably freak out from anxiety. By the way, when I say bed, I mean 1/2 inch plastic coated foam. That was worse than sleeping in many of my "outdoor" stays in yards and on sidewalks.

The worst part about that jail stay was not having any idea what time it was. Time seemed to take forever. I felt like crap; I didn't know when I was going to get to eat; and no one would tell me anything about my future, so I just sat and worried, alone in a cell.

Chapter 6

Hospitalizations for Alcohol Poisoning

That wasn't the only time I had tried to "break out." I broke out of the hospital. There is a reason I say "break out," because when a person is in the hospital for alcohol poisoning, the sick person not allowed to leave. My clothes were taken, and "anything else I might hurt myself with." I had to stay long enough to have rid my body of all the alcohol.

I've been hospitalized at least seven times for alcohol poisoning. I probably should be dead by now when I consider my hospitalizations and the near-death seizure from trying to quit. I would usually wake up in a hospital bed with an IV in my arm. The IV pinched and hurt and my first thoughts were "I guess I did it again" and "I wonder when they'll let me go." The reason for the IV was to get fluids into my body and get the alcohol out.

One time when I was hospitalized in Reston, I had a very painful treatment. When someone's body has been as sick as mine and it has been depleted of vitamins for months or longer, there is little potassium left. Low potassium levels cause severe muscle cramping. Body fluids become completely out of balance. The treatment was to put back the potassium, by the bag, through the IV needle stuck in my arm. The IV needle reminded me of a fancy toothpick stuck in a sandwich. The potassium replenishment is quite painful. Most people get a bag or two.

On a slow drip a bag of potassium can last for about two hours. It hurt in a "skin on fire" sort of sting from my hand to the base of my neck. I opted for the fast drip, more painful, but I just wanted to get it over with. We started with two bags. Then the nurse came back with another two bags, and then another two bags. That's 6 hours on the fast drip trip of pain. Finally, she came back one last time telling me the doctor ordered two more bags. By this time I thought he was punishing me. It hurt so badly I couldn't sleep, and to ease the stinging I chose to hold ice bags on my shoulder. I held the ice bags for eight hours or more, alone in a hospital room. Nobody called me in the hospital. There was nobody who knew where I was, or what I was doing. I didn't tell anyone either. After a hospital stay, I'd just go home, not tell a soul, and easily slip into my same old pattern.

I'd like to thank that doctor. He cared enough about me to put me through a series of tests to see my internal organs for the first time. He told me I had a "bulb" on the end of my pancreas because it was irritated. I didn't know what the pancreas' job was in the body. I had pancreatitis, also known as inflammation of the pancreas. He told me I should never drink again. In fact, those were the doctor's orders written down on my medical release papers.

One leading cause of pancreatitis is heavy alcohol use. Anyone who already has had one episode of pancreatitis caused by alcohol should stop drinking entirely to prevent reoccurrence or becoming chronic. The doctor warned me that I was at risk for my pancreas to burst, and if that occurred he said I'd probably have diabetes the rest of my life. I continued to drink, even though I was scared just a little.

Then, I was in the hospital again. Since I really despised being held in the hospital, once I was alert, all I could think of was when I would get out. On this occasion, I saw that my clothes were nearby.

I yanked the IV out of my arm; obviously I still had that liquid courage running through my veins. I got dressed and walked out like I was any other person. I got all the way down to the lobby, and there was nobody around, until at the last moment a nurse passed me. I tried my best not to look at her, but as luck would have it, she recognized me. I ran for it! I broke out of that hospital like a horse in the Kentucky Derby. I ran out into the dark, not knowing where I was. I ran through the wet grass and just kept running for a long time. I was a runner. In my mind I'd figure out where I was sooner or later and just keep running all the way home or to where my car was last. Running a few miles or so wasn't a big deal. There was just a little part of me that was scared because it was night time, and I was out alone on the street. Since I was still inebriated, I couldn't judge how long I ran, or what exactly happened, but I know the police were called to haul me back in. After the rest of the "normal" routine, I got to go home after I was alcohol free.

While I make that story sound a little funny, as it was to me at the time, it was very serious. Alcohol poisoning can and does lead to death. Too much alcohol can directly impact the central nervous system, slowing breathing, reducing heart rate, and affect the natural gag reflex. That can lead to choking, slipping into a coma, or sometimes death. Vital organs (heart and lungs) can be slowed to the point of stopping. I should probably be dead by now.

I have been in the hospital seven times for alcohol poisoning. My first hospitalization was January 15, 2004 at Reston Hospital. My second and third hospitalizations for alcohol poisoning were on October 3, 2004 and October 9, 2004 at Reston Hospital.

Here is a rating scale of alcohol levels, increasing in

33

volume, and ending in death. This is how alcohol feels to most people at the various levels:

.02   Feeling mellow; slight body warmth; less inhibited.

.05   Noticeably relaxed; less alert; less self-focused; coordination impairment beginning.

.08   Drunk driving limit; definite impairment of coordination and judgment.

.10   Noisy and possibly embarrassing behavior; mood swings; slower reaction time.

.15   Impaired balance and movement; drunk.

.30   Many lose consciousness at this level.

.40   SOME PEOPLE DIE at this level and most lose consciousness.

.50   MANY PEOPLE DIE, at this level breathing stops.

On my trip November 22, 2004, to Loudoun Hospital, my blood alcohol was a .367. That is four times the "definite impairment" level, into the "most lose consciousness" area, and very near the "some die" level. That measure was taken after a period of transport and could have been higher. When a person gets enough alcohol in their body, breathing stops, and they die.

Looking back over the Loudoun medical tests, I had a high rating on the AST (SGOT) measure, which is a test to show the functioning of the liver. It turns out that this is a measure of a "fatty liver." The most common reason for a fatty liver is alcohol abuse. After that it's mostly due to liver disease, such as diabetes mellitus, obesity, or chronic hepatitis C. I felt like a schmuck for causing my body, specifically my liver, to be in trouble as if I had a disease or something. I couldn't believe that I was doing that to myself. I was hospitalized on April 22, 2005, for my alcohol withdrawal seizure, mentioned early in this book, at Inova Fair Oaks Hospital. I was there for four days.

Chapter 7

The Beginning of My Long, Relapsing Recovery

I met an incredible person, now my husband, Joseph Price, July 20, 2005. Considering he had only known me a few months, it was extremely evident that I needed rehabilitation for my addiction. I moved in with him almost immediately. We put most of my belongings into a storage unit, and I shared his room. I fell in love almost immediately with him. He was calm, steady, wise, and very good looking. Little did I know I was to marry a 'doctor' of sorts who loved to study people's behavior. Although he doesn't have any college degrees, he is filled with a wealth of information on personal development and psychology. He is well-studied in the Bible, and has given me a wealth of spiritual support.

A few months earlier, I had flown down to Florida to see my sister around June, 2005. She said, in the Fore-word of this book, that I was in awful physical shape. She described me as "looking like our father did when he was dying of alcoholism." She said I went to see her because I was reaching out for help. It was very clear to her that I wanted help, and that I needed help, but I didn't know what to do or how to stop. I tried to stay sober during my trip, but it was difficult. I brought just enough alcohol to keep me going and normal around her and my nephew and niece.

When I returned to Virginia, shortly after I met Joseph, I got arrested again. That is when my sister decided to take action. She rallied the family, and mustered the courage to call Joseph, and she asked for his help. At the same time, my brother had been researching rehabilitation facilities. Thank the Lord for all of these things coming together to save my life.

Joseph was willing to help get me to Florida, even though he knew it involved a small bit of trickery. I arrived by train in Tampa, Florida with my car in the back of the Amtrak. Of course, I practically drank the whole time. Not only did I drink from my stash (for off hours), but as soon as dinner was called, the wine would flow and make for a merry and funny trip. For an alcoholic this is an excellent way to travel, not to mention the fact that the drunk is not on the road driving and putting others at risk. If a person wants to be out of control all the time and yet not get a DUI or harm others, they've got to stay out of the driver's seat.

I had been drunk in the week preceding my "visit" to Tampa, so I had forgotten that I sent my remaining $8,000 savings to my sister. I had agreed to give it to her. As far under the influence as I was, I'd give my money away. I believe in my drunkenness I knew she was trying to help me. Deep in my heart, I knew I wanted to get back home near family for help and stability. I wanted to get back to normal. I wanted the old Karen back. I wanted to stop having to be tied to this drug, that, if I didn't have it, my body would revolt against me.

When I arrived on Saturday, my family had big plans for me. They took away all my belongings, and they put me on a 24 hour watch at a hotel, someone was always with me. My brother even let me have a couple beers that evening, which I promptly threw up in the hotel room. The family made me agree to just see this one doctor first thing

Monday morning. I didn't know why, and I was a little apprehensive, but I said I'd go. When we got there in the morning, we all went in one room, and I found out what it was all about. I was at a rehabilitation center, supposedly a pretty good one. As the doctor discussed the option of me staying there for a month, I cried. I wailed and burst out with a resounding "yes," that I'd do it. I loved my family so much at that moment. I loved them for caring, for tricking me, for working out the details, and for helping me to give me a chance to get my life back.

I was in rehab with a woman who had four DUIs. It surprised me that could happen in one person's lifetime. I wondered how long she had been drinking, since she was older than me by at least ten years. She was very devoted to the program, and was my roommate and my keeper of sorts. There were young guys and ladies with good upbringings that had other drug addictions. There was one famous athlete. There were also some people with similar backgrounds to me, what I call the "professionals gone bad." The PGB were educated, mid-life professionals, who because of their addictions were ready to be thrown out of ever having a career or a life again.

At the rehab, there was a rigorous schedule of daily activity from very early, 7 a.m. to 9 p.m. Several times per week we were allowed to go to A.A. meetings together with the more "senior" people who had been in there for months sober. By that time, they had received driving privileges, and were instructed to drive the rest of us when needed.

As a new person in this rehab, I was not allowed to carry any money. I was given money to shop at the grocery store every week and everything was monitored. If I wanted to walk across the street to the store, I had to go with a leader that carried my money. This part was very, very hard for me. It never even crossed my mind to try to buy alcohol, but maybe that was the point. It would have been impossible. They had to make it impossible.

I shared a room in a house that had two twin beds and a dresser for each of us. The house was run like a military unit with leaders and jobs to do. I could get in trouble for being late, not doing chores, sleeping in, missing my ride to the center, or for not going to an early morning session to talk about my feelings or read from the Alcoholics Anonymous book.

I was happy that I was getting healthy and sober. I was unhappy about not being able to go look for a job, call my boyfriend, Joseph, who was still back in Maryland, or even get on the Internet. I did cheat and call Joseph from the house phone once or twice even though I wasn't allowed to use the phone. I wrote him a letter almost every day. He wrote to me, and I loved his letters. I saved them, and I still have them. They are very special to me.

One thing about me though is I'm a penny pincher. I was brought up that way and I've been known to be one of the cheapest people around, which also makes a person quite self sufficient and a quick learner. Why pay someone to do something for you when you can do it yourself? What I really was paying for, in my mind, was to break the physical addiction. Well, I started really feeling good after a couple days. They gave me medication that allowed me to get by without drinking, yet kept me from having a seizure and life-threatening withdrawal. It's a methodical amount of benzodiazepines for certain. As I was slowly weaned, I began to feel better and better. I felt human again and normal. I loved not having alcohol around and not needing it. I loved not needing to figure out where I hid my stash to stop the morning shakes.

My skin looked better. My face looked better. I felt stronger. After about two weeks I was rid of my physical dependence. They gave me a certificate that said so. To me, what a glorious day! All that for a mere $5,000! When my sister told me, at about two weeks into it, that rehab cost that much so far, I decided to leave rehab early. There

38

was no way I would let my brothers and sister spend my last pennies I had for that rehab center after I was already "fixed." If they did, how would I survive after I was out, with no apartment, no job, and no money?

I recall the day I made the decision to leave. As I stood out front of the center, there was a beautiful blue sky and a warm sun. It was such a pleasant-looking sky. The center Director was on my right, and my sister, holding her baby, was on my left. The pressure was incredible. I looked toward the sky, as if I were looking for God to give me a sign. I looked to the heavens, it was beautiful, I did feel peace and sureness. I really stared upward for quite a while, focusing, and only barely hearing the two of them asking me questions that I left hanging unanswered. Finally, I turned my face from that beautiful sky, not really getting a sign, and I said "I'll leave Monday." That was in a two days.

I recall the last days before I left. The people who run the rehab had tried to have the other addicts pressure me into staying, and the staff took every chance they could to verbally stop me. They all took it upon themselves to have little talks with me, to try to persuade me to stay. I was very uncomfortable. The more I said "no," the more I was also unwelcome there. Everything was hunky-dory while I chimed along with the program, but once they could not control me by making me stay, they feared me. The also feared that whatever I had going on in my head would spread and others would get the idea to leave.

Now I'm still not sure if a few more thousand dollars and two more weeks would have made a big difference in my future. I don't think so, and here's why.

Rehab wasn't the solution for me. It was a learning experience that helped, and it certainly got me straight for a while. The best part is that I got medical care to stop the chemical dependency. It also introduced me to God through the 12 steps. Although I hadn't made a real spiritual connection, I was learning to look to Him for help. For me though, I needed a really big reason to quit drinking, to quit being irresponsible, and to stop ruining my own life. My husband called this having "a big enough why," which means having a big enough reason why to stop. That reason would come later.

The chemical dependency was broken and gone, but there were issues with getting down to the core reason of why I drank, and I needed to figure out how to deal with the core problems. I had a really nice couple of months after that, but just months after rehab I started drinking again. Here was my rationale, and my problem. I wanted to prove to myself that I could drink socially; to prove I could just have a few light drinks and then call it a night. I wanted to prove that I had control. I proved myself wrong.

I have to make a major point here. This is the biggest reason alcoholics fail. They get an idea in their head that just one, or just once, one night, they can drink. It's not okay. One drink is too many, and one drink is not enough. Total abstinence is the key. I know there are books out there that will try to convince a person how to be a social drinker or reach a goal of drinking in moderation. There are books that provide a plan to reach a goal of drinking in moderation, while prescribing herbs, vitamins and prescription medication to stop the craving.

That's too risky to try, and it's risking life for the problem drinker or alcoholic. I think about it, and think back. One drink leads to two. One night of having a drink leads to two nights. What was okay on the weekend becomes okay during the week also. Next thing you know, I'm showing up at work with a hangover and everyone can tell. I don't really have to spell out where it ends. It ends with me losing my job, and then having even more ammunition to drink, like lots of time on my hands, anger, and depression.

Chapter 8

Mental Health Laws

Slowly but surely, I started drinking again. I would go on drinking binges. Something would upset me, and my solution was to have a drink to calm down and not let anything bother me. I usually didn't plan to get drunk, but that's what always happened. My binges would get worse and worse. In essence, I was relapsing. For me, one relapse after my first few months sober led to many more, and by then I didn't even think of them as relapses anymore. If a person is drunk more than sober, they must have the opposite, like I did, relapses of sober periods.

On one binge, I became extremely out of control. As it turns out, I was put into the hospital under the Baker Act. It was the same day that news came out of former Tampa Bay Buccaneer's Coach's son killing himself, December 22, 2005. In Tampa, Florida, that was a catalyst to take this type of self-inflicted hazard more seriously. Alcoholism is a type of suicide. It's easy to kill yourself with alcohol slowly or quickly. I was definitely hurting myself. I don't think I wanted to be here on the planet with everyone else much more. I asked God to let me go. I dared God to strike me down with lightening or anything else that would end my seemingly pitiful life. In fact, I should be dead by now based on statistics.

Laws are really different from state to state. I had

no idea. Being a drunk up in Virginia, I thought that things were easier for a drunk in Florida. Florida state didn't own the liquor stores, and there was a booming private enterprise system at work with a liquor store on seemingly every corner there. I could buy alcohol late into the night, maybe all night, except for not before noon on Sunday. That's interesting. So an alcoholic only has to minimally plan ahead on Saturdays only, or stay boozed up enough to make it through to noon Sunday. That's how alcoholics think.

What I didn't know about Florida, is that they can pick me up anywhere, including at my own home, if someone thinks I'm are a danger to myself. The Baker Act, put into law originally in 1972, is the Florida Mental Health Act. It is supposed to be used when a person shows signs of mental illness and meets criteria for voluntary or involuntary admission for medical help. Usually the person presents a threat to themselves or to others. Approximately 7,500 people are taken into custody under the Baker Act each year[2].

Newer legislation, signed in 2004, reformed the State's mental illness law. At that time Florida had been one of only nine states that didn't provide for involuntary outpatient treatment. Statistics show that having outpatient treatment reduces the burden on law enforcement, reduces hospitalizations, reduces homelessness, and reduces arrests and incarcerations. Not only does this Act reduce the previously named costs to the community, but it helps people who are sick, and ruining otherwise happy, productive lives.

Just out of the hospital only a few weeks, I was drinking often, daily. January 18, 2006, I went to jail. I didn't just "pass go and go straight to jail" either. I passed by the hospital. I was incoherent enough that the officers thought I had taken massive amounts of drugs to commit suicide.

I don't remember much. At the police station, having been propped up while blacked out, I was seated in one of those cheap industrial chairs. Not surprisingly, I fell out of the chair and landed with my face on the hard linoleum floor. The police took me to the hospital, and I don't remember any of it. They gave me some x-rays of my cervical spine. I suffered a fat bloody lip laceration but was otherwise okay. I'm glad I didn't break my neck.

I was blacked out. That means I was functioning but not consciously functioning. I lacked short term memory capability. I have since read the documents that the doctors wrote from that occasion, things they said I said, and I don't remember any of it. I'm not sure when I was taken back to jail. I finally "woke up" much later. I woke up walking around in a large holding area. I was booked and stayed overnight. On the one hand, I'm sort of happy to know what it's like. I've always been one to try new things. To me it was like getting to be a criminal for a day, without really being one. It was sort of like it is on TV. The other women did scare me. I tried not to talk too much, but rather fit in by muttering small complaints about the food or whatever.

Chapter 9

My Spiritual Awakening

Along my way in life, through all of this challenge, I had begun to grow spiritually. In my growth, I have had some major shifts occur that I will call turning points, leaps of faith, or better yet, leaps into faith.

There was a period of time during 2006 when I didn't have a job. My car got repossessed because I lost my job and hadn't built enough savings up. I rode my bicycle everywhere, or walked, or took the city bus.

I walked to the grocery store and carried a big backpack. Whatever wouldn't fit in the pack, I'd carry in my hands. It was about a half mile walk to the grocery store. I enjoyed the exercise and actually wished people weren't so dependent on driving everywhere.

One summer day, late in the evening, when I was walking by this tiny little church that I passed many times, I heard wonderful sounds of beautiful voices singing. It was a very rickety building and most people passing by in their cars never even noticed it. It sits on a prominent road, Fowler Avenue, just east of 50th street in Tampa. The name at the time was Miracle City Worship Center, a non-denominational place of worship with about a 98% African American membership. Since I didn't mention it before, I'm white, Caucasian, of European decent, fair-skinned, or whatever.

I had been drinking a little that day. I went into the church. The singing and the awesome spiritual power inside was something I'd never experienced before in my life. Sure, I had gone to church, but it was nothing like this! I asked the usher if she would hold my backpack of groceries in the office. I'm sure that was an odd request. I don't know if they looked at me strangely; I wasn't paying attention to that. I was the only white person in there, but that didn't bother me. At that moment I knew I needed this kind of excitement and glory in my life. I needed to share what these people were sharing. The positive energy and love was incredible as the entire church body seemed to move together in praise. I didn't realize I had been there before.

Prior to that, months earlier, I had stopped into that church the same day I bought a Christmas tree. I had been drinking a lot that day. I barely remember. I walked into the church and sat down carefully and quietly into one of the back pews. I had not been inside a church in more than a few years. As I sat there, an overwhelming feeling came over me. Everything was rushing over me, thoughts of how my life was ruined, deep sadness, hollow emptiness. I laid my head in my shaking hands and I cried. I sobbed and wailed, with my shoulders lunging up and down with each outpour. At that moment, I didn't care who saw me or what else was happening. It all rushed over me at once.

I felt a pureness pierce the center of my body. I was reaching out to God for help. Every part of my body was pleading for God's help and love. I felt loved at that moment, and it was as if I had to break down completely right then and there in order to receive it.

Several women of the church came to me and held me, comforting me. They asked if I was okay. All I could say was "I'm drunk." What I meant was that I am drunk, I have a problem, and it is costing me everything I love. I need help, and I'm crying out for it. This was the first time I felt love from people who didn't even know me. They paid no attention to my drunkenness invading their holy place. They held me and offered me some food. They helped me out of the sanctuary and I, walking slow and hunched over, went with them to another room. I was given a plate of a wonderful southern-cooked dinner. Quite suddenly, I came back to my senses, and realizing I was standing in a room full of people I didn't know, I became scared and very aware of my surroundings. I hurried out, with the only thought on my mind of getting home where I belonged with Joseph.

While attending that church over the next year, I learned that in the Bible there are words of wisdom about worrying. On one Sunday, the preacher dwelled on the subject of worry. I learned that it's a sin to worry. A profound lesson became ingrained in me, but it would take time to make its full impact. What I came to fully understand later is that worrying is not having faith. Worrying is not putting faith into God. It is denying God of his power and presence and of all that He is, and all that the He can do. He is almighty. Nothing is impossible for God.

Now, whenever I start to think about what's going to happen, later today, tomorrow, or next month, I remind myself that worrying is a sin, and then I make a conscious effort and I stop worrying. I turn the situation over to the Lord. I put everything into God's hands. It's that simple.

As for biblical references to drinking alcohol, one can look up a lot of that information on the Internet. There are a handful of specific references about drinking alcohol. It likens drunkenness with gluttony. It also says that whoever is intoxicated by it is not wise, and it warns to not become drunk or to become enslaved by drink. What stayed with me most was that the Bible says that the drinker of alcohol will be poor.

"For drunkards and gluttons become poor, and drowsiness clothes them in rags." Proverbs 23:21

I had tried to quit many times, but nothing ever impacted me like the power of God and the strength of the church. I was getting closer to God and Jesus Christ, and I was getting stronger. I learned to love myself and then I learned to love something more. As I alluded to earlier, I had to have something to love more in order to beat my demon. It was going to take something incredible.

Chapter 10

The Longest Functional Blackout

I was delusional and if anyone who saw me babbling on would have thought I was crazy. I had blacked out for over two weeks beginning July 13, 2006. That's just the point, when people black out, they don't know how long it was or anything they did. Months later in 2006, I called one of the authors of "The Alcohol Blackout: Walking, Talking, Unconscious & Lethal,"[3] Dr. Donal F. Sweeney about my blackout.

As far as we ascertained, I may have had the longest black out period of his knowledge. Someone like me, in an alcoholic blackout, can fully function. I could walk, talk, sign agreements or contracts, and write checks. I have two memories of the black out period.

I was with my neighbors, shopping at a well known low price department store. My neighbors were certainly not my friends as it turns out. They helped keep me drunk for much of the time, as they swindled me and spent my money. Anyway, on this occasion, they put me in one of those handicap driving shopping carts at the store. He showed me how to drive it. I know I wasn't doing a very good job of driving it. I was periodically coherent, for less than a minute at a time.

Suddenly, I had collapsed and fallen off the scooter to the floor. When I awoke, I was lying on the floor looking up at a store manager's face that was obviously seriously scared and concerned. There was a group of people around me. I didn't know anyone. It's quite shocking when I "come to," and only for a minute I'm conscious and find myself lying on the floor with a bunch of people I don't know standing in a circle around me.

I assured the manager I was okay. Then I was mentally absent again. I was again back into my blackout. I bought some clothes that weeks later I would find didn't come close to fitting me, and I left with my neighbors. I still wonder how is it possible that I could tell everyone I was okay, brush myself off, and continue to shop like nothing was wrong. Was this a common thing?

I can hear it now over the loud speaker "Ccccrrrrck," "Uh, Bob, we've got another one passed out in aisle nine, can you see if she needs some help with breathing or anything?"

The second memory I have during that two-week period is of being completely delusional in my house alone. Again, I have no idea of time between these days of fleeting consciousness. I was on the floor in my office at home. I peered around the room, and I thought I was somewhere else. I thought I was at my neighbor's house. As I slowly scanned the room, I recognized some of my personal belongings. My first thought was that this guy stole my diploma and printer. I proceeded to pick up the home phone and call my own cell phone, which was very near me. I left myself a message that I would hear a couple weeks later. The message was of course that I was at my neighbor's house and I was telling my husband Joseph that the guy had stolen my stuff.

Part 2

Recovery

Chapter 11

A Major Turning Point

It was hard to keep track of time because I was indoors for several days. I spent a couple days at the hospital recovering, and then I was released sort of "under the custody of a clinic."

I had to go to a publicly funded clinic because I didn't have any health insurance. The name of it is Baylife Mental Health Center, in Tampa, Florida. This was worse than jail for me. At Baylife, I was in a small 15 x 15 room with very hard plastic chairs. They kept the temperature very cold. I would guess the temperature from the air conditioning put the room at what felt like about 60 degrees. Each of us without a jacket was practically freezing. They did give out sheets, so I asked for two.

There were about a dozen other people in that room with me, along with the security officer. The people there ranged from crazy and dangerous to suicidal. In fact, we were all there because someone thought we were suicidal. Some just showed more evidence than others, like the girl next to me who had slit both her wrists and was bandaged up to the elbows. She seemed normal except for the visual clues on her arms. She's the only one I talked to because I was afraid of everyone in there, but like I said, she was right next to me. Certainly there was no reason to acknowledge the really loud, constant-talking, swearing, angry, crazy guy that smelled so badly he made my stomach turn. If I even acknowledged that guy, it would only fuel his outbursts, and possibly invite a barrage of angry words toward me.

There was a TV encased in Plexiglas so that no one could injure themselves on it or use it as a weapon, for example using a shard of broken glass. We were stuck in that room forever it seemed. I was allowed to make a phone call, but I had to ask. When it was meal time we all walked in a line to the dining hall and had whatever was given to us. Most of us were afraid to sit with anyone, for fear of striking up a conversation with someone really unpredictable. We ate without talking, and when everyone was done, we walked back in a line to the holding room.

Hours went by and I guess it was night time according to the clock and the one window which no more light came in. Dare I sleep? Would someone try to touch me or hurt me? Slowly each of us quietly chose a spot on the floor to lay down. It was the hardest and coldest floor I'd ever slept on. In college, when I was really poor, I didn't have a mattress, so I slept on a boarded box spring with a couple layers of sleeping a bag and a comforter on it. That was hard, but it was nothing compared to the freezing floor at Baylife.

Before dozing off, the nurse gave me a dose of a drug that is a benzodiazepine. She was concerned if I didn't take it I might have a seizure, and obviously she didn't want that on her shift. I wanted the medicine too, and it helped me sleep.

I was in there for about 24 - 36 hours. I'm really not sure. The point was that we were being monitored and held until a medical practitioner could evaluate us. That evaluation would determine whether I could go home, or if I'd have to stay indefinitely because I was deemed mentally ill and a danger to myself. We had to wait until "office hours" when the doctors and nurses would come in, and then I'd get my turn to be interviewed for my sanity level.

What I was worried about is that supposedly I had told the officers who came to get me originally at home that I wanted to kill myself. I might have said that, although I denied it. I was really concerned that if I had said it, I would be held indefinitely in a psychiatric ward there at Baylife.

One of the things they do, to gather information, is call the family or people who were witness to the incident that got the person there. I finally got a call through to Joseph and tried to tell him in code not to let on if I had said I'd hurt myself. I just knew staying in there would be intolerable, and I was ready to do anything to get back home. I finally got my interview.

First, I learned about the results of my blood tests from the nurse. The nurse told me, as she looked over my hospital stay medical records, about how bad my body was degenerated. Yes, me the marathon runner. The girl who ran three miles almost every morning for ten years; I was the snowboarder, skier, sailor, cyclist, marathon runner, and MBA graduate.

I was scared to death, really. It was the second time a medical professional looked at my tests and pointed out just exactly what I had been doing to my body. She pointed out all kinds of medical reasons I had to get help. I was really sick and killing myself slowly.

I had been slowly robbing my bones and teeth of calcium. My bone marrow was suffering. Many of my body functions were at risk. My body was depleted of many important nutrients. That's why my skin looked awful, kind of yellowish with a lack of any other color. My eyes were off-white, not like the whiteness of a babies new eyes. I couldn't get solid food down at all; it just wouldn't pass my throat anymore. I really found it hard to swallow anything except liquid. When I tried to take a vitamin, I had to chew it up. I also had red splotches on my skin. What appeared to be psoriasis had been on my legs and arms for a few years now. It was embarrassing and I almost never wore shorts or skirts. I had a multitude of bruises at the time, and the clinic took pictures to protect themselves from liability.

I had the option at that moment to listen to her and get more help, or just get the heck out of there. She had spoken with Joseph. I could have just been released and gone home. Because I always cared about my body and health overall, and that Baylife nurse knew how to really get me thinking about it, she said she thought she could try to "get me a bed" at a facility if I would sign the papers to "Marchman Act" myself. First, what a great sales technique, by telling me it was hard to get a spot, already wanting help, I thought this was something I definitely needed to get. It wouldn't cost me any money, and they'd help me get better. I loved and missed Joseph, but dear Lord I wanted to stop this madness. For the rest of my life I would remember this nurse, her serious demeanor yet caring undertones. If I had her name, I would add it near the top of the list of people who helped save my life. Thank you.

Chapter 12

Staying In When the Going Got Tough

The nurse explained to me that the Marchman Act (Substance Abuse Impairment, Chapter 397, F.S.) meant that I was voluntarily admitting myself for treatment. I signed my life away. That was really hard to do. So for the second time I put my life into the hands of professionals in August of 2006, the first time being rehab in October 2005. This was different though, I was locked in 24 hours per day, 7 days a week.

I took this offer because I was now finally afraid of dying and sober enough to understand that medically I was really killing myself. Much of the focus before had just been on how alcohol was ruining my life. I know that it really struck a nerve in me when a medical person told me how badly I was damaging my body. That was a major difference for me from past decision-making about drinking or not drinking. This time I did it because I didn't want to die.

By the way, if a person doesn't admit themselves, then under the Marchman Act, a spouse or guardian, any relative, a director of a licensed service provider, a private practitioner, or any three adults who have personal knowledge of a person's substance abuse impairment can put them away. For minors, parents can do it.

On the website of A.C.T.S. it explains under "services," under "Marchman Act Services" the following paragraph:

"The Marchman Act provides for assessment, stabilization and treatment for individuals who are severely impaired due to substance abuse, are refusing voluntary treatment and who meet the following criteria: He/she is likely to inflict harm on self or others and/or His/her judgment is so impaired due to substance abuse that he/she is incapable of appreciating the need for care and of making a rational decision regarding that need for care."

A.C.T.S. is the Agency for Community Treatment Services, Inc. in Tampa, Florida. I agreed to go to A.C.T.S. I thought I would get to see Joseph. I had called, and I was planning to have him meet me there before I put myself into their care. It had crossed my mind to just leave with Joseph and not go in. I wanted so much to be back with him. Over the course of only a few short hours, I did a 180 degree turn and fully changed my mind. That was it; I was going to nix the treatment center and get back home with Joseph as soon as possible.

Well, that's not how it went. I was securely and carefully transported and escorted into the building. I had already signed the papers, so I couldn't have gotten away anyway. In fact, to my complete shock, once I went in the door of A.C.T.S., I was locked in like a jail. Once again, I went into a panic. I couldn't believe my life was not in my own hands again. I was under a camera in a small waiting area. When the intake coordinator arrived, I tried to tell her that I didn't want to go in, that I changed my mind. It didn't matter, and inside I felt my heart drop to my heels. I felt sick not knowing where I was, where I was going, what it would be like inside, and how long I would be there. After the last place I was in, I had reason to be extremely afraid.

To my surprise, I had a bed. Okay, it was more of a cot, smaller than a twin-sized bed, but it was soft and it had blankets and a pillow. I was given a toothbrush, toothpaste, shampoo, and soap, and I could even take a shower alone behind a curtain.

While there I didn't get to talk to Joseph at all. There was a pay phone, but Joseph never answered. I feared I had lost him. Little did I know, he told me later that he actually considered leaving me and heading back to Maryland, or at least just getting away from me. He didn't though. He gave me another chance.

While I was at A.C.T.S., I also had to get screened by a psychiatrist. That made me very nervous, because if I didn't "pass" who knows what would happen to me. The thought of going to a mental ward, not having my freedom, and losing Joseph was enough to scare me silly. Five days later they let me go home. My psychological interview had gone fine. I had been given medication for my blood pressure and benzodiazepines again to help bring me down out of the alcohol. That plus the hospital time made me physically stable.

Something else at A.C.T.S. impacted me greatly. On Sunday, a preacher and assistant from a nearby church came to the facility to hold prayer service. No one had to attend, but a handful of us did. We sat outdoors yet within the fence. They had made little rows of chairs separated by a narrow aisle. The preacher stood at the front and with gripping emotion provided us with her words of wisdom from the Bible and her life. She was like us, and she had come out of her addictions. Through the grace of God, she regained her own life, and as she spoke, she filled me with hope. I wept and held the hand of my friend J.C. while he wept also. I was so grateful for this preacher to come to tell us of hope and the love of the Lord. She showed me it was possible, and showed me a way out.

I got home on August 7, 2006. I count my days of

sobriety from August 1, 2006, my last hospitalization, and I did in fact reach one year not drinking a drop. I didn't go to an A.A. meeting to pick up a one year chip. It didn't seem like something I had to do. I realized that I had quit, and that I didn't need to make a big deal out of it. By celebrating a year, it seemed to continue to give power to the alcohol.

It seemed to me the more people celebrated years of not touching it, the more they recognized it as a lingering part of their life. It was as if alcohol haunted their lives and, like the predator watching its prey it hung around in the shadows just out of sight waiting to be given the right chance again. I did get a little tired of going to A.A. meetings. It seemed to give power to alcohol. Some people I met seemed so unhappy, like everyday was still a huge battle with the demon. Some "old timers" would make harsh remarks to me about how I was doing my program. They told me not to talk to men. They told me to get a sponsor. Then they chastised me for not getting a sponsor or missing meetings. I couldn't connect with that. I had moved past that, beyond the stage of "I'm still fighting it." I took it a step further and psychologically did not even acknowledge alcohol anymore. It was simply not part of my life. It was only a part of my past. Later, I would discover that I was also using a technique similar to one called "Feelization" to psychologically break free and separate the two parts of my life.

Chapter 13

My Big Reason to Quit

Dozing off to sleep one evening in early September, my husband and I had pulled the covers snugly around us and we began to drift away into slumber. I had been quiet all day about it. I couldn't wait another day, and I certainly couldn't sleep. I was also very afraid of what I had to tell my husband. "I'm pregnant," I whispered twice. He rolled over, and pretended to fall asleep, a slumber that actually took much longer to reach than anticipated.

I had never planned to have children because I didn't know how those women stopped drinking for 9 months. I also wanted complete freedom and very little responsibility. However, because of my blackout at the end of July, leading to my second medical intervention and rehabilitation, I had stopped taking my birth control pills. So, the first time Joseph and I made love about a week or so after I got home, our beautiful daughter, Savanna, was conceived back in mid-August. That was God's handiwork.

Other women have told me that being pregnant or breastfeeding didn't stop them from their drinking. There is no way I would jeopardize my baby. It was one thing to hurt myself, but I couldn't hurt this little person, a gift from God, growing inside me.

I know I didn't quit drinking for my family, because I could not see the hurt I caused them. Only after I was pregnant, and had been sober for many months, did I realize that being a drunk had been a very selfish act, and killing oneself is a selfish act. Only then did I realize that if I started living my life loving others, then suicide was something I could never do. I also couldn't use the "installment plan" to death that alcohol offered. If a person love's their family, they simply can't live like an alcoholic. I love my daughter more than anything on earth. That was my first step to quitting drinking. I was filled with joy, and in church every Sunday became more special. I prayed a lot. My belly was getting bigger and rounder, and so was my heart.

God is love. I didn't understand that ever before. I've learned and I believe, that my path was laid out long before I was born. I had to go through many tough times to achieve a love and appreciation for God, life, and love. I knew that with God, I could get through anything. If I put God first in my life, then everything else would be as it should.

"But seek first His kingdom and His righteousness, and all these things will be given to you as well." Mathew 6:33

Now, not only was I taking care of my own body and mind, but I had someone else growing inside me. I had to get a job somehow. It was extremely difficult. I had such a shady couple of years, and I was way out of the loop for networking.

I went on more than one interview pregnant. I didn't lie and try to say I wasn't pregnant. I told the truth, that I was expecting a baby in May. Many times I did not get the interview, and the interviews I got didn't lead to jobs. I know it was because of my pregnancy. Right when I needed a job most, I couldn't get one. So I made a web site, and then another one, and more websites after that to earn money. I really couldn't get enough sales to make that work as a viable business or income. We were struggling financially and just barely getting by.

My husband made enough money to keep us going in our little two-bedroom apartment for a mere $675 per month and he took care of our other expenses. I spent only $40 dollars per week on groceries. Mostly we ate a lot of sandwiches, soup, eggs, and potatoes. Luckily, by the grace of God, a community resource program helped pay for Savanna's birth. We had no savings whatsoever. I thanked the Lord, my family, and the community for taking care of the birth of our baby.

"And we know that all things work together for good to those who love God, to those who are the called according to His purpose. Romans 8:28

I finally landed one job that allowed me to work from home as a Search Engine Optimization Specialist along with doing my own business of creating small web sites. It felt great to be working, learning, making progress, and simply living again. Finally, baby Savanna was born in May of 2007.

Soon after her birth, I stepped out to interview once again. I had to earn more money to be able to pay for day-care at $900 per month. I was so overweight at around 150 pounds, that I had only one jacket to wear to the interview. It was a maternity jacket I bought for interviewing when I was pregnant. I couldn't stand the thought of raising our little girl in that tiny apartment. I had owned so many houses before, and I took it all for granted. Now I just wished I could own any home. It seemed impossible.

Once again, I was given a chance. I had an interview for Account Manager at a Tampa website development company. Before I walked in the door that day, I slowed my walk and began to pray to God. I asked Him if it was His will that I land the job, then so be it. I wasn't going to try to land the job really. I walked in with the mindset that it had already been decided, and that I was just going to go through the motions and I would just see what the outcome would be. I had learned to have faith in God. I learned to put my life in God's hands, where it belongs and resides.

That company took a chance on me. Obviously they knew I'd just had a baby, but they must have seen my incredible desire, and I had the experience to do the job. It was hard to go to work everyday and miss my daughter. Most women don't go to work two weeks after the baby is born. Most women I know have jobs that allow them to stay home for some period of weeks and are guaranteed to have a job back, by law.

Because of my years of alcoholism I would have a lot of hard work ahead of me. I received the best gift in the world, my daughter, and my biggest challenge was making sure she would have a good upbringing. I couldn't regain the money I spent in those years of drinking. What I could do though, was work harder than I ever had before. While writing this book, I hoped that the proceeds would help me raise my daughter and help her through college. Maybe we'd even own a home completely by the time I was sixty, so that Savanna didn't have to take care of her parents and she could get a good start in life.

Once again, through the glory of God and my faith, I was led down the path to a program in the community that helps people get into owning a home. It simply amazed me how, if I set my sights on something, and prayed, then it would come to be. For all I know, having an incredible aura of determination and hope was the biggest factor. I was able to buy a perfect home through the program. I can hardly believe it myself, but my wishes and dreams were coming to fruition.

What had I learned, and what had consistently been the center of all this positive? My trust and faith in our Lord God gave me all the strength I needed. He gave me the strength to move forward without worry. He knows I live my life loving Him, and for that He gives me the greatest gifts. The gifts may come not only in the form a house or car, but the greatest gifts are breathing, living, loving, and sharing. The other wonderful gifts are gratitude, humbleness, and knowing that He saved me.

Part 3

How I Quit Drinking

Chapter 14

I Simply Quit Drinking

If you skipped ahead to this chapter to get the big secret key to quitting drinking, here it is. Quitting drinking, for me, was a combination of two things. The first is that I had to have a reason to live, and my reason was given to me by God. That is my daughter Savanna. The other thing is something about me that is not unique to me, but difficult to reach. A doctor would have to explain it, probably a psychologist or psychiatrist. I quit drinking because I had a new beginning, a relationship with God, and a few simple rules. That is how I quit being an alcoholic and regained my life. I can tell you how to stop. I will have two simple rules, and they are all that counts to simply quit drinking. Any person can quit using those two actions, along with some soul searching, and considering letting God be a part of their life. If a person turns his life over to God as it should be, and follows His path, all things will come together as they should.

The two simple rules are "don't pick up the bottle," and "take it one day at a time." It is so simple you wouldn't believe it. It's like walking a mile, just keep picking your feet up and putting them down and don't stop. If a person never picks up alcohol, then they certainly can't drink it. When not drinking is achieved all day today, and then they go to sleep, and if they get up tomorrow, and repeat it, then it's done. It's like the movie "Groundhog Day." Just do it once, and then keep doing it every day you wake up. You may also want to thank the Lord each day that you wake up.

About me though, I have a character trait that many people have pointed out to me over my entire life. I have a "switch" in my mind that works like this: When I make up my mind to do something, it is going to get done. It takes something powerful to make that switch turn on, but I know what does it or how it happens. I have incredible determination. Someone once bought me a gift that was one of those framed definitions, and it was absolutely perfect for me. It was a picture of a runner, and the word "Determination." The definition read, "The race is not always to the swift, but to those who keep running."

I do challenge every doctor, psychiatrist, psychologist, researcher, and personal development expert to answer how I did it. It takes a mind doctor to tell about how that "determination" switch works. The definition of determination is "the act of deciding definitely and firmly" and also as "firm or fixed intention to achieve a desired end."

For example, I told my husband I wanted to write a book this year. Then I told him I was definitely going to do it. I started the book one morning after thinking about how best to accomplish it. Since I have a 9-month old, a full time job, and a "side" business, let alone grocery shopping, laundry and cooking, how would it be possible? I decided to follow advice, and I set aside a time everyday to write. I got up at 4:30 or 5:00 a.m. everyday, and I wrote at least 1,000 words per day before getting ready for work. It actually doesn't matter how long this took to write, but that I did it. It took much longer to reveal the final book with carefully reconsidered words and chapter order, but committing to doing the writing everyday is called determination, persistence, and discipline. It's about focusing

70

on a goal, and making a set of actions that will achieve it. When all the little actions are completed, that goal will be reached. Now, other than the advice I've given above, I have only a few other tips to share.

For alcoholics among us who scoff at the idea that it is as simple as it has been presented, not only by me, but in the reference books, let me give a few other examples of how simplicity is the key. Note, I didn't say it was easy. I said "simply quit drinking."

How do people who can't walk start walking again? They take one step, the first step, possibly partial steps, or maybe just lifting a leg. How will my little daughter learn to take her first steps and walk? She'll crawl; then she'll slowly start to pick herself up using objects to hold herself steady; next she'll walk while I help her; one day, she'll take her first step on her own, and walk.

It's a process and dedication, along with determination. Just don't pick up a drink. It's really that simple. All of life can be broken down into simple little tasks, and better yet, simple little decisions. Don't succumb to the thought of buying the alcohol; stop from going to the store; don't have alcohol on hand; don't open any bottle or can of alcohol; don't raise it to your mouth; don't swallow it.

I ran a marathon in much the same way. One doesn't just go out one day and run 26.2 miles, which took me 4 hours and 23 minutes. It starts with a step. I had been a runner for much of my life. For a decade or more I regularly ran 3 miles per day. I saw a posting on the Internet that if I would run the marathon and raise money for a group fighting Neurofibromatosis, then they would give me a ticket to run in the 2002 Disney Marathon and a hotel room for the night. I followed a training plan, the same plan many follow. Slowly I built up the miles and trained my body to be able to go the distance required.

I also completed college and graduate school in the same way. It's as simple as having the goal set in my mind, and doing one thing after the next toward reaching it. Once I finish a class, or a semester, I take another, until I'm done. Anyone can teach themselves that reaching goals is that simple. I taught myself to break down a large task into small steps. With alcohol it is the same idea, I break down the goal of not "picking up" into the little decisions and actions that make up the sequence that get me the desired result.

Chapter 15

Alcoholics Anonymous: A Spiritual Foundation for Recovery –Twelve Steps

My favorite part of A.A. was the 12 steps, a spiritual foundation for recovery. Not only did learning the 12 steps give me my spiritual foundation, but more importantly, it has given me the incredible gift of a centered, grounded life. I have a peaceful soul now. I believe I walk in the path the Lord has laid out for me. He is almighty, and He gives me the strength to live a peaceful life because I believe in his omnipresence, power, and love.

There have been many new A.A. attendees that are scared away at their first meeting because of the deep spiritual foundation the group is based on. People who stay with A.A. learn that they are not in charge of their life, which is a basic premise of Alcoholics Anonymous.

When attending A.A. meetings, a person finds that they have to say these things as the first step to recovery as follows. Admit that your life has become unmanageable, and come to believe that a Power higher than yourself can restore sanity. They make the decision to turn their life over to God, or however they see their Higher Power. They become humble and ask God for forgiveness and to remove shortcomings. They pray and meditate to improve conscious contact with God, and pray for knowledge of His will. They also make amends and seek to take a personal inventory. **Last, they hope for a spiritual awakening.** When the spiritual awakening comes, it's a duty to carry the message to alcoholics however and wherever possible. This book, for me, is the twelfth step. I am fulfilling that step without knowing that would be the outcome. I didn't plan to do that, but I feel so strongly about helping alcoholics, that I am writing my story to share.

Since most people don't have a reason to pick up a copy of "Alcoholics Anonymous," it is full of anonymous stories similar to mine. I've read some stories that are worse than mine, some people ended up prostituting themselves or being homeless. Again, I thank the Lord, and my family for saving me.

Dr. William D. Silkworth, in the preface of "Alcoholics Anonymous"[3] writes this, that the alcoholic won't quit "unless this person can experience an entire psychic change." He also writes, "On the other hand – and as strange as this may seem to those who do not understand – once a psychic change has occurred, the very same person who seemed doomed, who had so many problems he despaired of ever solving them, suddenly finds himself easily able to control his desire for alcohol, with the only effort necessary being that he is required to follow **a few simple rules**."[3] This reminds me of way in the beginning of adulthood, and at the beginning of this book, how I kept myself from being an alcoholic with a "few simple rules."

Other than the psychic change, and a few simple rules, Dr. Silkworth also notes, "In nearly all cases, their ideals must be grounded in a Power greater than themselves..."[3] I came to believe in God and Jesus Christ, something much greater than myself. God is love, and love is greater than any desire. It's that simple.

If asked what my "psychic change" was, I'd say it

was a culmination of several things. I was afraid I was going to lose Joseph, and I didn't want to die either, along with a new found love for the baby growing in me, and developing faith in God. I really do love myself enough not to let myself do something as stupid as get caught up in that downward spiral again. I agree with Dr. Silkworth in that it is easy to control the desire to drink. In fact, I don't even think about it. I've rewired myself to associate drinking with feeling sick and out of control, neither of which sound very appealing.

I also agree with statements made in the Big Book about having to clear the alcoholic's mind before he can be reasoned with. Those who have pulled themselves out of physical dependence, which usually requires hospitalization and treatment, afterwards, believe in themselves and "still more in the Power which pulls chronic alcoholics back from the gates of death."[3]

In the end, my problem with alcohol was worked out by spiritual means, after regaining my body. I needed a doctor to fix my body, but I needed the teachings and the love of the church to make me whole. I have a much greater wellness level having been through this long tragedy. With my spiritual growth, I have learned to really enjoy life, and all of the gifts in life at the simplest level, like waking up, smiling, laughing, and helping others.

Chapter 16

My Trademark Technique – Mindset Reversion

I use what I call "Mindset Reversion," which is reverting to a previously held mindset. It is different from "Feelization" in that it extends beyond it. "Feelization" is feeling an experience over again, reliving through feeling. Mindset Reversion extends all the way into returning to a mindset from a particular period of time. However, my mind doesn't completely revert back to the mind at, for example, childhood. I focus on a particular time's mindset about a particular thing. This technique I find useful in long-term alcoholism recovery.

Defined, "mindset" means "a mental attitude or inclination, a fixed state of mind" and "reversion" means "a return to a former condition." Hence, my definition of my trademark technique "Mindset Reversion" is reverting to a previously held state of mind or mindset.

In psychology, it is somewhat similar to visualization or using imagery, also called mental rehearsal, or mental practice, which is a technique used by athletes. Visualization had formerly been used where an athlete visualizes watching (in third person) himself win a race, for example.

Slightly different, "Feelization," is a newer

approach. Dr. John Eliot, a psychologist, described "Feelization" as visualizing from the first-person perspective, as opposed to the third-person view that was used in classic visualization tactics. In "Feelization" a person attempts to feel the desired experience to attain as opposed to seeing the outcome they hope to achieve. If the person has already had the feeling before, then mentally they take themselves back to that place in time and relive the feeling.

I take it one step further. More than visualizing and feeling, I also recall my mindset from an earlier time. I revert back to my previous mindset as it relates to alcohol. That is the basis of my "Mindset Reversion" technique. I relive a time, by using all my senses to recreate the experience of that time of life. In my case, I simply think back to another time, and then how I *thought* at that time. Mindset Reversion is about tapping into what your conscious thoughts were at that time of life.

I remind myself first that there was a day when I didn't drink everyday. I think about what those days were like. I think about what my life was like. I was happy for the most part, healthy, and certainly managing my life well. I think about how I would start any given day with a jog, checking email, and preparing for work. Next, I mentally travel back in time farther to a time in my life when I hardly drank, like just on the weekend nights going out dancing. I recall many days of getting up and going to work and school and leading a normal almost "hum drum" kind of life. Although it was not super exciting, it was definitely stable and I have good memories. Next, I think back further to a time when I didn't drink alcohol at all. I find myself reliving that time and recapturing that mindset and outloook. I realize that it was completely possible for me to never think of alcohol or drinking at all. It was simply not part of my life or conscious thought processes.

This mental process of reliving a certain time's

mindset allows me to relive what it was like to not know the feeling of being drunk. It allows me to feel like I did then – to be absolutely oblivious to alcohol. To really go back that far I have to think back to when I was a teenager. I think back to high school, and maybe some brief time periods during college.

This reliving of the mental state allows me to forget all about drinking. I begin putting my mind into a different time. I can feel the difference. It feels refreshing, clear, and un-tempted by the pull of alcohol. ***That is the best moment, when I remember when there was no alcohol in my life***. Now, I simply release the thoughts of how drinking feels, and I revert back to a time when there was no alcohol, and no alcohol problems, and no feeling of being intoxicated. I go back to a time of not knowing what alcohol felt like. Furthermore, there simply was no alcohol. Now, I hold that mindset in the present; there IS no alcohol.

As I write this, I have not ever been hypnotized, nor do I know much about it. I suspect, that getting hypnotized may be similar to what I just described. Some people prescribe herbs and hypnosis as a path to abstinence or controlled drinking.

For me there is no such thing as controlled drinking. Why? Because if I drank, it would remind me of how much I loved the feeling of alcohol. I don't want to remember that it felt good. I make a practice of not remembering what alcohol felt like. I focus on remembering that it made me out of control and set back from being in touch with my senses, numbed. I have re-associated my thoughts of alcohol to be tied to unhappiness, feeling out of control, and unable to take care of myself. All that negative association works for me.

In fact, I've used the same technique to lose weight. I reassign the feeling of eating a sugary sweet treat to a negative feeling of my heart rate increasing, a short burst of energy, followed by a bad low blood sugar level, and then a craving for more sugar. I trained myself to look at sweet foods (and a few other foods like pasta and breads) and think about how they make me feel when I eat them. I focus on the negative. After going through this a few times or a for a couple weeks, I have reprogrammed my mind to have a negative reaction, associated with a negative physical feeling.

If it is difficult to understand, get a doctor to help. I'm certain there are doctors who know what I'm talking about and different ways to do it. I encourage anyone to try it.

Most importantly, if a person has not ever had alcohol, I suggest not trying it. No one knows ahead of time if they will be one who will simply love it too much. Rather than trying it, just don't. **Let my story warn of just how dangerous and narrow the line can be between a drink and a drunk.**

Chapter 17

The Drug Alcohol – Not the Best Medicine for Anxiety

It took a long time for me to find out that I have Generalized Anxiety Disorder. It is very common among alcoholics. It's quite simple how they are related. I drank to numb my feelings, mostly my fears, and stop my brain from worrying about everything or thinking too fast. Many people with anxiety disorders drink alcohol.

Alcohol is a readily available, inexpensive, legal drug that people can get at almost any store at any hour and immediately reduce and relieve the symptoms of anxiety.

If a person has trouble with going to a party, and they think they need to drink in order to "loosen up" to be able to talk to people, they need to find another solution. There are many ways to work this problem out. Like learning to ride a bicycle, it's hard to start, but just keep trying. A person may have to thrust them self into the mix without alcohol many times, and eventually prove to themselves that they don't need alcohol in order to have fun talking to people. It takes practice, and may involve working on areas of self esteem, confidence, and possibly getting "centered." There is also prescription medication that can help.

I took part in a study at the University of South Florida for Generalized Anxiety Disorder. They gave free medicine to study the effects and determine it's viability to market the drug. For me, it was great. It did provide me with some relief from anxiety. But that wasn't enough. When the study was almost over, I broke down and drank. I showed up at my last appointment after drinking a bit. They did all the regular tests. When I left that day, the doctors were supposed to prescribe something to take the place of what I had been on. Unfortunately for me, I'm not sure what happened. I started taking Paxil and went wacky. I also started drinking. I had a few weeks of extreme problems and lost another job.

People can see a psychologist and therapist to get the tools to work on self esteem and confidence. They can see a dentist if they have crooked teeth. People can see a nutritionist or read books to gain the knowledge to lose weight (another confidence crusher). A dermatologist or family doctor can prescribe medicine for acne. If someone wants, or really needs, medication to help with emotional difficulties, it's best to see a psychiatrist. Finally, in order to "fix" one's mind and state of being, consider a personal development expert. Most importantly, for the ultimate change, go to church, read the Bible, and learn to grow faith in God.

As for the anxiety, I learned to cope from the Bible. I learned that my mental "position" can make a difference in how I approach everything. I had to learn to listen and change how I talked to myself; this is also called your "inner conversation." I grew spiritually to strengthen how I view the world and not worry so much. I also learned from personal development that I could have the power to control my thoughts and actions. I learned to stop being reactive, and put everything into the right perspective.

Chapter 18

Personal Development

Personal Development professionals have a special place in the world of available help. With personal development and my spiritual growth, I am now an amazingly centered and strong person. Once a person makes a decision to quit drinking, and they are medically and physically able to stop, they've got to get their life back together. They're a mess. Courage is gone. Personally, I felt worthless. It took me a long time to get to the bottom, and it took a long time to dig back out. Even writing this book was part of the process. I had to come to terms with acknowledging my past, to grow enough to help others, and to not be embarrassed.

Personal development professionals can help in the process of rebounding and rebuilding. Mentally a person has to start "owning" their life again, maybe even more than they ever took ownership and responsibility before. In fact, there is a lot of lost time to make up for, so get geared up. It's the right time to learn to think positively, and not dwell on recent failures. For me, it was the perfect time to work with some experts in psychiatry, therapy, and personal development to uncover the reasons why I drank alcohol to begin with. During the time that I was no longer physically dependant, but I was binge drinking throughout most of 2006, it was because I was using alcohol to deal with feelings.

What causes a person to drink is called a "trigger." Discovering what triggered my drinking was very important. Because I have learned my trigger, I can get my defenses ready and change my mind in how I handle a triggering situation.

My trigger is anxiety, coupled with a feeling of a lack of love. In the past, a bad relationship where I wasn't getting enough love or attention easily sent me to the bottle to feel better on any given evening. Once I had enough alcohol in my system, I started feeling better. I'd go out and talk to a lot of people and have a blast. A stressful day, or stress in my life causing anxiety and worry is definitely when I wanted to drink to ease that pain. My mind thinks very quickly, kind of on a "turbo speed" level. I used to worry too much. I guess I'd call it "a mind on worry at turbo speed." My goal was to slow down my brain. Alcohol did the trick wonderfully.

Now, that isn't an option. I have found ways to cope. It's important that I don't let my stress level get to high, and that I deal with anxiety some other way. I cured the loneliness, by marrying my husband, Joseph, and by having our daughter Savanna. He is a wonderful husband who is home every night, never out drinking with the guys, and I'm very happy to have him each and every day. Savanna fills my day with love and joy. But in reality, I recently realized that I'm still alone.

Therefore, I have only myself and God. While at first I was scared by this thought, I realized it is okay. I share my life and love with the people around me, but just as each of us enters this world alone, we will leave it alone. One day I will stand before the Lord at the gates of Heaven, and it will be just me and Him. That is a somewhat uncomfortable thought that I am learning to deal with, just the same as I wonder if I will outlive my family members or not. Will I be here more alone?

Chapter 19

How Joseph Learned to Help

What was it about my future husband that made him care enough about someone else to make a difference? One can go to the age old discussion of nurture versus nature that develops our self, how we act, and how we get our basic makeup. However, by the time a person is middle age, I think they've decided just who they are. They've taken what they were given, added all of their life situations and encounters, and out of that decided what to keep and what to get rid of.

Joseph Price just so happened to be a person who had taught himself using personal development for over twenty years. He took what he was given growing up, love and strong biblical learning, and he added a lot of positive influence and reading, to make himself a great person. I firmly believe that because of this, he stuck with me and helped me get out from under my battle with alcohol. It was his "eye" of experience that saw something inside me that shouldn't die. He has told me several times that when he first met me, that there was something inside me that was special.

Personal development is about always growing and always learning. Joseph had made a commitment to himself early on in life to continually develop and grow spiritually and mentally, and he believes that giving to others is the best gift of all. Because of that, he was exactly the kind of person who cared enough to help me, and I was someone who really wanted and needed help.

The most important things that shaped Joseph were his years of studying people. I really do consider him a behavior scientist. I don't care that he didn't finish high school. That doesn't matter. He took a simple job as a cab driver and turned it into a venue for a scientific study of people. He wasn't just mindlessly driving them around; he took a real interest in watching, listening, and learning. As a midnight cab driver in Washington D.C. he saw people from all different walks of life on a daily basis. He saw people in all manner of states of unhappiness, hurrying, worrying, and yet also saw some people very calm, collected, and unstressed. He took note and tried to understand, and he developed a compassion for people's circumstances. Many people were not getting the results they desired or the life they dreamed of having. Then he made it a life mission to help people. He calls it "leaving someone better off than when they came" into your life.

For over twenty years my husband Joseph has read everything he could get his hands on, and listened to all the tapes he could, about personal development. He is a walking library of knowledge on the subject. Because of it, he may be a little hard to live with due to the constant teachings, but his knowledge is solid, and it has helped me form a higher level of commitment to living a life with purpose.

It's no surprise that when he met me, he knew he should help me. What a huge burden to take on though. I believe that his desire to see others succeed and lead happy, satisfied lives stepped in and gave him the strong willingness to help put me back on my feet again. He hardly knew me, but when my sister called him, he took on the challenge. I'm not the first person Joseph has "saved" or "helped." He has been helping people with their struggles all his life by sharing his knowledge, compassion, and love. Everyday now I return the favor to him with my love and support.

Part 4

Loving An Alcoholic

By Joseph Price, husband

Chapter 20

Loving an Alcoholic

By Joseph Price

Karen's period of drunkenness, which lasted for almost two years of my own life, was one of the hardest times of my whole life. I'd like to forget about everything, every bit of pain and turmoil during that time. However, as a person that is committed to helping people reach their full potential and experience more in their lives, I've chosen to abandon what is comfortable for me. Once more, I'd just as soon forget about that whole period of time, which was a living nightmare. It's difficult for me to go back in time to talk about that span of life, but, now that I have released that, I will share my story of loving an alcoholic.

I don't think it will come as a big surprise that the day I met Karen she was under the influence of alcohol. I actually met her as a result of holding a door open for her at a mall, Thursday, July 20th 2006, at 5:30 p.m. to be exact. I'm a very precise kind of person. I'm a direct, precise, no nonsense guy. With me, what you see is what you get. With a slight slurring, Karen started making general conversation with me. As she was doing that, I was preparing to make a great departure on my own merry way. I saw some pain, some serious pain, and I saw someone who needed some real help. I slowed my walk and talked to her a bit more. Somehow, moving past her problems, we made a connection. It's something I can't explain, but there was a connection of some sort. So I talked to her a few more minutes before I left. We exchanged phone numbers 21st-century style, where you call the person's mobile phone number while you're standing together, and then you save it to your phone list. After I left, I thought about her, and I said to myself that she had too many issues, and I would not be calling her. However, God had something else in mind.

After we parted ways, Karen lost her phone in that mall. The next day, my phone rang, and I answered to hear a nice gentleman calling from Karen's phone. He had found the lost phone in the parking lot somewhere. Since I was the last number dialed on that phone, he called me. Fairly sure I didn't want to have any part in meeting Karen again, I told him to leave it a restaurant that she mentioned she frequented. However, the restaurant wasn't open that early in the morning, so he told me he would leave it at a hotel nearby.

My conscience got to me, and I realized that the phone needed a little intervention, if it was going to get into the hands of it's owner again. I was busy that Friday, so it was a matter that I'd deal with on Saturday. I was a professional driver, and was very good with directions and details. I remembered where Karen said she lived, and for some reason she had given me her apartment number. I am really passionate about people losing cell phones; It's not usually the lost phone, but the forever lost phone numbers and connections to others that is most damaging.

On Saturday I carefully knocked on her door, just hoping to return the phone and get a delighted response. To my surprise, she answered the door in the same inebriated state that I left her in two days ago. I was shocked. I thought, how was it possible that she was still toasted. I stayed a while, observing Karen as we talked about nothing much. As time passed she became a little more coherent. She offered to buy me dinner as a thank you, and I carefully accepted.

Slowly a relationship began. Behind all the nonsense Karen displayed, I saw something great in her, and she saw something in me. We became good friends quickly and subsequently lovers.

About ten days into our friendship, I definitively knew that Karen had a very serious problem. Not ever seeing this sort of behavior, I contacted one of my best friends for advice. Shawn, a recovering alcoholic with more than 15 years of sobriety, spoke to me about what could be done to prevent Karen from hurting herself. She was clearly more than out of control and needed help. At that point, after seeing her outrageous behavior, and after talking to my dear friend who had suffered similarly for years, I knew what I was dealing with. At that time, most people would have ended the relationship. Fortunately for Karen, I'm not most people. Shawn told me that in Virginia there is nothing a person can do for someone who could harm themselves in the manner Karen was doing it. There wasn't any way to have the authorities get involved.

Distraught, and finding myself caring for her more than planned, I made a decision. In my mind, there was a person, a child of God before me, with a demonstrated potential of killing herself. I just wasn't going to have that. I committed myself, without realizing it at the time, to do whatever was necessary to find some help for Karen. I would do whatever it took. The word commitment has a much different meaning to me than for many others of our society. To me it means going all the way, no turning back, all retreat avenues cut off, and get the heck out of my way because there are no other options.

About a week later Karen moved in with me. I wanted her to be close to me. She had admitted her problem to me more than a few times. I thought that I could lead her to making her own extreme commitment, and she could be done with it. I was like most people though, ignorant as hell about the power alcohol can have over a person, even though they want to change their self-destructive behavior.

I believed, having studied human behavior for most of my life, and I knew that people are capable of overcoming extremely difficult challenges. It's all about change. Change happens in an instant. Change really happens in just an instant, even though most people don't think so. Getting ready for a change is what takes time; that could take a lifetime. The "prelude to change" is a long drawn out struggle. Change happens when a person is ready and they decide they want to change. Until that critical point, it's a struggle of wavering commitment and teetering decision-making. Karen's "prelude to change" was years in the making, and I stayed along side her, as painful as it was for me.

One thing about both me and Karen, is that we are caretakers by nature, and we like to do things for others. Karen was good at being a caretaker for me. She would often cook wonderful meals. However, not only was she cooking, as in dinner, but she was cooking herself into being drunk.

We had a kitchen that was fairly closed off at one end of the house, and she would drink when she was in the kitchen. She was good at hiding her alcohol, and for her the kitchen was a great place to sneak a drink unnoticed. She hid a box of wine in a cupboard. The kind of wine that comes in the box with a little spout at the bottom, so a person doesn't have to pick it up and pour it. She would open the cupboard, and slip her glass under the spout to carefully and quietly seep the wine along the inside of the glass, so as not to draw any attention to her actions. I realized was what was going on, and I started to fear that she was going to burn the house down. I thought she might leave

94

the stove on. By the time she was done cooking, she was always blasted. She didn't have the capacity to see what kind of a complete mess she had made, so I would clean up after her all the time.

My room was upstairs, and each time she cooked, she would put the entire meal on a serving tray to carry it all upstairs. Inevitably, she would trip on the last step and spill the food everywhere. That happened a lot, and it usually happened right before I could get to her, even though at the very first creek of a step I'd jump to try to help her.

We lived with my roommate for about two months. My roommate quickly tired of her behavior. She'd pass out all over the house, fall asleep on the bathroom floor, or be found in the bathtub. My roommate said she had to go.

About that same time, Stephanie, Karen's sister, recognized that Karen needed intervention. Often Karen would call her sister up while drunk and ranting and raving. Stephanie, who also wrote the foreword of this book, got together with her brothers to figure out how to help.

Stephanie was able to get my phone number, and she called me and went over her perception of the situation. When Stephanie called me, she suggested that Karen should go into a rehabilitation center. When asked, I recall saying, "Yes, she needs rehab, and she needs rehab now."

Together, we made arrangements to send Karen back to Florida. Karen thought she was just moving back to Florida to stay with Stephanie for a while. It took about 10 or 12 days to accomplish getting Karen ready to leave. She didn't want to go. I needed her to leave because my roommate had been my friend for years, and she had stressed our long-standing friendship. Finally, Karen got in her car, took some belongings, and went to the auto train to take herself to Florida. I knew she was sad and broken-hearted. She was lost. She was fighting for her life, and drinking away all her thoughts and emotions. I knew it was hard for her to leave me. She actually had no where else to go except to her family in Florida.

She was gone away from me to another state 900 miles away. "Thank God, peace again," I thought. Right then, most normal people would have said to themselves, "great, she's gone and I can clean my house up and go on about my business." We had only been together a couple months. It would have been easy for me to get over her, and I'd never date a person that drank alcohol ever again. However, I guess I'm not like most people, and there was always something special that I saw in Karen. I always had a sense of hope. I felt in my spirit that she would come around eventually. She seemed too good to be wasting away.

We didn't talk much in October. She was in rehab; rehab was going to fix her. Rehab would be a magical solution to all her problems. She was supposed to be at the rehabilitation facility for 30 days.

When Karen was completely sober, after a couple weeks, her sister told her that it was Karen's own money that was used to pay for the rehab. So far $5,000 had been spent. Karen immediately decided she didn't need anymore of that kind of rehab and she left. For about two weeks after that all of our conversations on the phone were good. She seemed very sober and lucid. I of course felt that she was okay.

She is a good saleswoman by nature, and she really convinced me that she was okay. I decided to take a big chance. Not happy about my current work in the limousine and professional driving business, I knew I was still cheating myself of living up to my own potential. I wanted to pursue my lifelong dream to be a positive force in touching many people's lives, by getting into the professional speaking industry.

I was ready to move somewhere different. As long as I lived in Washington, D.C., I feared I would probably never get out of the transportation industry because I was

96

good at my job and many considered me one of the best. My clients loved me. I was very personable and conscientious. I had a lot of clients.

I looked at moving to Florida as a good opportunity to make a change. I believed in Karen. I thought she had made the necessary transformation.

I began preparing to move to Florida, so I started my goodbyes to friends and family. Before leaving D.C., I took a weekend trip with my older daughter, since I would be much farther away after the move. She was in college. We took a little trip to Atlantic City. It was hard saying bye to friends I'd known for such a long time.

Later that week, Karen called me and she was intoxicated. She had just gotten into some kind of argument with her father. She was in a drunken stupor. I thought, "oh no, what is going to happen, and what am I getting into"? Here we go again. As usual, I believed in her. I didn't like the way things sounded, so I hopped on a plane to Florida. She was supposed to meet me at the airport. She didn't make it to the airport. I took a cab to her apartment where I found her in bed drunk.

I thought to myself, "this is just one little phase of relapse." One thing I've learned about alcoholism is that sometimes part of a person's journey to transformation includes a bout with relapse. Many people, when they begin the journey, which may start with rehab, sometime in the process have relapses. I wrote it off as that, and she was able to moderately drink and not get out of control.

My hope was so great that I did move to Florida to be with her. The day I was supposed to move, Karen was to fly up to Maryland. She missed her plane, but eventually caught a later flight. When she did finally arrive she was clearly intoxicated. That would have been a good time for me to just get her to go back home to Florida and leave it at that. I still hung in there and moved to Florida.

I drove the U-Haul truck with my town car in tow.

Karen was trying to have a "clean" start with me. I know she was really trying. However, she had to drink so badly that she resorted to drinking mouthwash. While we drove to Florida she was vomiting the whole way. As it turns out, she learned the trick of drinking mouthwash from reading a chapter of a book by the famous author Stephen King, who admittedly drank mouthwash during his alcoholic years.

As soon as we got to Florida, we met my oldest daughter in Tampa, and the three of us drove to my mother's house in South Carolina for Thanksgiving. That whole weekend Karen didn't drink anything. I thought everything was going to be okay. Then, the next week, something happened and it started up again. Whenever she used to drink, especially when she started drink less, whenever she would just take one drink then she would become a raving drunk. She would go on a week-long binge. Most of the time, it ended up with some kind of trouble. Sometimes when she was drunk she would call 911. Most of the time the sheriffs would come to the house, and they would take her to the hospital to have her looked after. This one time when she called, she must have mouthed off to the 911 operator or said something more extreme than usual, and the law enforcement officials that came had her "Baker Acted."

The Baker Act in Florida allows the authorities to take a person to a mental heath facility for observation if it is perceived that they represent a threat to themselves or others. This actually happened just a couple days before Christmas. "Merry Christmas," honey. They held her for a couple days for observation and they released her early because of Christmas. She was sober for the next couple of weeks until the shock of being in a mental health facility wore off. In January, she started up again. There was a rage and weeks of the same rampage went on and on.

I was very scared. I knew that sooner or later she was going to have a bigger problem. I was always worried when she went out. She would wait until I went to bed, or when she thought I was asleep, and she'd go down the street to the local bar. I worried that she might not make it home.

Karen liked to drink all different kinds of alcohol, but there was one in particular that whenever she bought this brand of beer, that she would be worse than usual. I came home one evening, and I saw an empty six pack of this beer. I knew there was going to be trouble. Sure enough, I got a call from the jail. She had gotten a DUI. The court process would take months, and in the meantime Karen landed a good job and was working. She also began to take part in a study of Generalized Anxiety Disorder being conducted at the University of South Florida. She was going to their bi-weekly research meetings. She was taking the medication, and they were studying the effects. She seemed happy and less anxious, really normal.

Karen wanted to get married. We did get married, quietly, downtown at the Clerk's office on April 27th. She had been holding a good job and not drinking. We went on a three-day cruise, and low and behold, she drank like a fish. We argued and it definitely got ugly. I couldn't believe it, now we were married and she had gone off her rocker on the "honeymoon."

We got back, and she returned to work. Everything was okay until the anxiety study ended. She got off the medication, and they had to give her something else since the study was over. They weren't going to just leave her to suffer a withdrawal. They prescribed Paxil, a popular anti-depressant that is also used to treat anxiety. It's not supposed to be taken with alcohol. I'm not sure what happened, whether she stopped taking the Paxil first or if she started drinking, but the combination was lethal. She was out of control, didn't show up at work for several days, and lost her job. Regardless of the fact that she had a signed letter from her doctors saying she had suffered a series of panic attacks, the company still let her go.

In May of 2006, she finally got her driving privileges revoked from the State of Florida for her January 2006 DUI. She didn't own a car anymore, and she was on probation. Since she didn't have a job, she opted to do all her community hours, rather then "buy them out" as people with money do. Basically, a person has the option to not do community hours and pay a fee instead. Not only did she do all her hours, but she also chose to work off her penalty fine too. One of the requirements of her probation was to not drink. During that time she followed the rules and had her monthly check-ins with her probation officer. She'd walk to the bus stop out front of our apartment and take the hour-long bus ride downtown, to see her probation officer, plus pay the probation appointment fee.

For those months she was fine. It seems that when she had to follow rules, she did so. Maybe it was only because not having her license, her freedom, and paying all those fines that she kept to the "no drinking" rule. She told me her goal was to get done with probation as fast as possible.

It seemed as soon as probation was over, and there were no more reasons to not drink, she started again. Since she couldn't drive, she rode her bicycle to the store to buy groceries, which always included copious amounts of alcohol to be stowed away in hiding places.

In July of 2006, my oldest daughter came for another visit. Karen kept it together all week so as not to embarrass me. At the end of the week though, she let her pent up frustration get the best of her, and she started on the worst binge of her life. It was actually the beginning of the end.

I didn't know Karen was in a drunken functional blackout. She was hanging out with the neighbors a lot. She would pass out in the grass out front at times. I was later told that even a Sheriffs deputy that lived across

100

the way brought her upstairs to our apartment one day. At that point, things were really out of control. For over two weeks, Karen was in an alcohol blackout, and I had no idea. She just seemed drunk, but I had no idea that she was operating absolutely unconsciously.

She was walking, talking, and doing normal things. I had to "child proof" the house because she would stumble often and get hurt on tables and things. One day, I checked her bank account online. She had gone to the beach with the neighbors, and I realized that all her money was gone. The money we had saved from when she was working was gone. I couldn't believe it. Several thousand dollars were missing.

A couple of days later, I came home from work one day to find her mumbling a bunch of gibberish. She was completely disoriented. She was more that just a complete mess; she was acting as if she was in a state of psychosis or worse. For example, she was talking about getting out of the car, when she was sitting on the floor in the kitchen. She didn't know where she was. Earlier in this book, Karen talks about a day when she called herself and left a message totally disoriented at home thinking she was somewhere else. That was the day. I had enough. **It was July 31, 2006.**

Chapter 21

How I Helped My Wife Simply Quit Drinking

By Joseph Price

    The mental health laws of Florida allowed me to finally assist in getting Karen much needed help. I called the police, and I used the Baker Act to have her hospitalized. This time though, she wouldn't just be staying for a couple days. This time she was going to have to go back to some sort of facility for observation, medical attention, psychological evaluation, and no idea of when she would be allowed to be out on her own again. She wouldn't know, nor would I know, when she would be "free" again.

    It was extremely difficult. I almost left Karen. I had been through more than enough pain and suffering. I was beginning to lose hope. It had all just been too much for too long with no definitive end or solution in sight. Karen tried contacting me from the various facilities, but I avoided her, and that hurt too. I really struggled. I cried, and I couldn't shake the sick feeling I had inside of either leaving her for good, or ever having to deal with this crap the rest of my life.

    Karen was under the watch of psychiatrists, nurses, counselors, and God while she went through the system under the law. She was kept, treated, and observed for a week at three different facilities, from July 31st until Sunday, August 7th.

When Karen finally was released from A.C.T.S., after she went there under the Marchman Act, of her own decision, she came out looking different. It was as if a real breakthrough of some sort had occurred. I knew she was different. At the time I couldn't pinpoint what exactly had changed. Later I found out that the Pastor of a local church had gone to A.C.T.S. to lead a worship service on that Sunday morning. Perhaps that was when Karen made the final decision, with God's loving presence, to stop.

She really had finally quit. It was hard to believe, and I have to admit, in the back of my mind I wondered when she would start up again. We were happy together and life was peaceful. After she was home for at least a week we made love. Two weeks later, Karen whispered in my ear, just as we were dozing off, "I'm pregnant."

Life was good ever since. Karen never drank a drop while pregnant. She has been a loving mother and a wonderful wife. She worked relentlessly to write this book amidst everything else she does as an employee, wife and mother.

I share in her desire to tell the story and make it known just how severe alcoholism is, not only for the individual, but for the people around the alcoholic, the chaos and disruption that the people around alcoholics face.

Epilogue

by Joseph

If you are a drinker now, your life is out of control, and you know if it is or not deep down inside, now is the time to take action. Enroll somebody to get on your team to help you through. No matter who you are somebody is depending on you and your need to shift your course so do something now.

Go to a meeting; talk to a pastor; talk to a friend; send us an e-mail. We want the best for you. If you are the family member of an alcoholic, don't stop loving them. Don't judge them; help them. Speak to your loved one's greatness, and forgive them for the stuff they messed up. Don't ever give up because the next attempt to help them just might be the one that takes them over the hump.

If you are a young person who has never had a drink of alcohol, don't ever take a drink. The best way to stop drinking, that I know of, is to never start. I hope this book and my contribution will make a difference in your life. Karen and I both share the desire to touch as many people as possible in a positive way. I support her and getting this book out to as many people as possible. Don't let alcohol and alcoholism win. Do something today to help and take action!

God bless,
Joseph F. Price
Apollo Beach, Florida

Epilogue

by Karen

I gained my life back along with a new found relationship with God. It is amazing that I can feel God's presence and sometimes seem to almost know my future before it happens. What I mean is, He fills me with a sureness, that, when I count on Him in the events and decisions in my life, it becomes very apparent to me that the path has already been chosen, and it is not actually a decision at all.

I am more successful now than I ever was. I have a business; I'm still doing websites, and working, but now I'm also consulting. My productivity and learning have increased exponentially. I have so much more time and stamina living an alcohol-free life. It is rejuvinating and wonderful.

Writing this book was worth any possible negative consequence in my career, because I have an important message that needs to get to non-alcoholics, problem drinkers, alcoholics among us, and to young people. Most important, I'm risking not being anonymous because I have to tell people what alcoholism is like, and I want to put a real face with this story of tragedy and hope. I don't want my story to be just a swept away secret in my past. I'm not afraid of my past anymore. I don't want alcoholism to be a "dirty little secret." That's how I kept it going so long, hiding it. I do not need to feel ashamed. *It can happen to anyone.*

My Higher Power is God. As for me, my trust and faith in our Lord God gives me all the strength I need. He gives me the strength to move forward without worry. I know that He knows I live my life loving Him, and I am so very thankful for all that He gives. He is with me everyday. Each day I pray, and I think of what I can do that day to show my appreciation and to use the talents He has given me. Everyday I think about His grace and love, and how I get to spend time with my beautiful daughter. At night, I pray that he continues to bless our family, and I often pray that he bring the same grace to others, and that they may know Him.

If you're having a struggle with alcohol, I want to tell you to stop today, right now. Don't pick up another drink of alcohol ever again. If my journey wasn't scary enough, do it for yourself and your family and friends who love you. Take God into your heart and really listen to the teachings of the Bible, then make some simple steps to start toward a greater life than you've ever known possible.

If you are struggling with addiction, **follow 'my program,' which is to put your life into the hands of a Higher Power, follow a simple set of rules, and use Mindset Reversion to learn to live alcohol-free again.** Think back to a time when you were free and happy; take yourself there again and simply quit drinking.

God bless,
Karen Price
Apollo Beach, Florida

References

1. Paton, Alexander and Touquet, Robin (4th edition) (2005) ABC of Alcohol. Wiley-Blackwell, Publisher

2. Houseman , Ceida and David (2003) Florida's Baker Act Fails Mentally Ill and Their Families," Tampa Tribune, April 6, 2003.

3. Sweeney, Donal F., M.D. (Author), with Liston, Robert A. (4th edition) (2001) The Alcohol Blackout: Walking, Talking, Unconscious & Lethal. Mnemosyne Press.

4. AA World Services, Inc. (4th edition) (2001) Alcoholics Anonymous Big Book.

ABOUT THE AUTHORS

Karen and Joseph Price have dedicated their business, Reaching Peak LLC, to providing inspirational and personal growth products and services worldwide.

The Reaching Peak Show
Tune into www.ReachingPeakShow.com for inspirational, educational, and motivational talk radio on the Internet with authors and speakers (podcasts available).

Reaching Speakers
Visit or become a member of www.ReachingSpeakers.com for author and speaker marketing services and training.

Reaching Peak LLC
Visit www.ReachingPeak.com, the company website, for what's happening, new projects, and inspirational products.

Reaching Peak Interactive
Visit www.ReachingPeakWeb.com for author and speaker interactive marketing services.

Karen Gregg Price
Visit www.AboutKarenPrice.com for information about Karen.

Joseph F. Price
Visit www.JosephFPrice.com for personal growth coaching or for an inspirational, motivational speaker for your organization.

Simply Quit Drinking
Visit the book web site at www.SimplyQuitDrinking.com for appearances, book signings, and other information.

The Challenge: visit www.SimpleChallenge.com to help others and raise awareness of the issues of alcoholism.

www.ingramcontent.com/pod-product-compliance
Lightning Source LLC
LaVergne TN
LVHW022317080426
835509LV00036B/2572